Coaching
Change

Thomas G. Bandy

Coaching Change

*Breaking Down Resistance,
Building Up Hope*

ABINGDON PRESS
NASHVILLE

COACHING CHANGE:
BREAKING DOWN RESISTANCE, BUILDING UP HOPE

Copyright © 2000 by Abingdon Press

This book is printed on recycled, acid-free, elemental-chlorine–free paper.

Library of Congress Cataloging-in-Publication Data

Bandy, Thomas G., 1950-
    Coaching change : breaking down resistance, building up hope / Thomas G. Bandy.
        p. cm.
    ISBN 0-687-09017-2 (alk. paper)
    1. Christian leadership. 2. Church renewal. 3. Coaching (Athletics)—Religious aspects—Christianity. I. Title.

BV652.1 .B35 2000
253—dc21

00-058267

04 05 06 07 08 09—10 9 8 7 6 5 4

MANUFACTURED IN THE UNITED STATES OF AMERICA

*To those many pastors and congregational leaders
who have a vision of their church
in the postmodern world,
and who are frustrated, overwhelmed, and exhausted*

*May this book give you
help, hope, and courage to try again.*

I express my deep gratitude
to my wife and family for their continued personal and
spiritual support,
and to my partners and colleagues in mission
for their patience, criticism, and prayers.

Contents

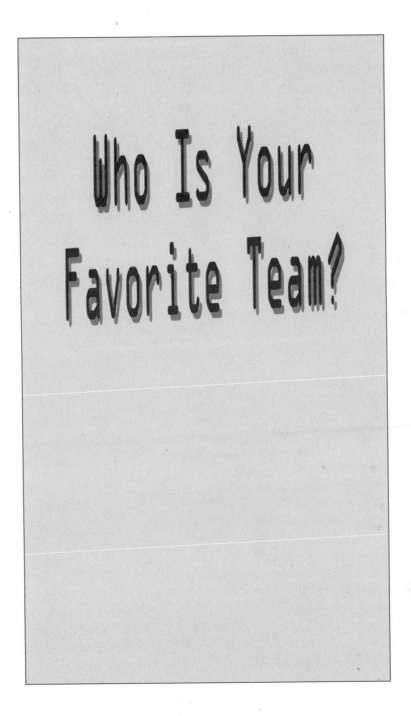

Ask people their favorite team, and they can tell you. They won't be offended. They won't hesitate. They will gladly tell you the reasons for their choice. They wear the cap, the coat, the jersey, and the shoes. They carry the backpack to school or have the bumper sticker on the car. The logo of their favorite team is everywhere.

Ask people their favorite church. Wouldn't it be great if they could tell you just as quickly and enthusiastically as they identify their favorite sports team?

Millennium people may also readily tell you their favorite band, their favorite school, their favorite restaurant, and their favorite charity. They probably decorate their cars, offices, homes, recreation rooms, and themselves with these logos, too. They volunteer time to raise money for these organizations, and sing the praises of their favorite "whatever" to anyone who will listen.

Wouldn't it be great if they could do as much for your church? Modern, twentieth-century church people may worry that such comparisons will trivialize the integrity of Christian faith. Such comparisons, however, recognize that in the new millennium more has changed than just the metaphors of organizational life. The very essence of organization and leadership has changed.

The reason millennium people are so pleased and excited to be associated with a favorite team (whether in sports, music, social service, or corporate business) is that they are experiencing organizational life and sharing organized leadership, in a whole new way.

Churches have been many things over the ages—commune, prayer group, parish, agency, corporation, and institution—but in the new millennium they need to be something else: a team.

There is no greater joy than to be a player
in the mission field of God.
There is no greater challenge than to be a coach
for a winning team.

Chapter One

What Is Coaching?

> Coaching is not about winning games. It's about growing winning people.

The Toronto Blue Jays of baseball's American League were in the midst of an impressive turnaround season. In the spring of 1999, they had been in last place. Nobody watched the games. Everybody scoffed at the young team. By August, however, the team was seven and a half games back of the division leading Yankees. These teams met for a key game that month. Pitcher Kelvim Escobar surrendered a leadoff home run in the very first inning. In the same inning, Escobar hung his curve ball too high and another Yankee hitter scored three more runs with another homer. Escobar was pulled out before he ever completed the second inning. The Yankees won the game 8-3.

The Blue Jays pitching coach was seen in what was politely described as "animated conversation" with Escobar in the dugout all during the second inning. Yet the coach appeared remarkably calm talking to reporters after the game. What did he say to Escobar? "Oh, I was just telling him that in a game like this you've got to go out there and be ready. He might have been doing that and just had a bad day, but I was just reinforcing that thought" (*Toronto Star*).

Despite the disappointing game, the reporters found the rest of the team remarkably relaxed. Having watched one of their best pitchers exit the game within two innings, the catcher said: "You know, our pitching's gotten a lot better. Our team is a lot better."

There are many books available about coaching written by enormously successful coaches. These are coaches who have won national sports championships and who are now applying the same principles and tactics to everything from business to religion. Many of their principles and strategies are helpful. Unfortunately, they are all oriented toward "winning." They help clients (businesses or churches) compete to become the best in the community, country, or world by raising the most money or attracting the most people. The "winningest" coaches in sports franchise history help other institutions become the winningest organizations in their profession.

However, coaching is not really about winning. It is about growing. Great coaching has more to do with losing without despair and doing better the next time without naïveté. Great coaching has more to do with clarity of purpose than achieving victory. Great coaching is not about winning the Super Bowl, but about empowering your players to resist celebrating victory with cocaine, fast cars, braggadocio, and lucrative endorsements, so that they can play again even better. More than this, great coaching is about losing a big game and empowering your players to resist steroid abuse, fast cars, despondency, and lucrative litigation with club ownership, so that they can play again better next time.

The great winning coaches are right in perceiving a connection between sports and every other human organizational activity, including the church. They are wrong in thinking that the connection is about achieving competitive success. The real connection is that sports epitomize the crucible of hope and fear that may be hidden, but is no less real, in all organizational life. Winning first place and gaining abundant life are not at all the same thing, but both professional athletes and television "couch potatoes" always seem to miss this crucial fact. Why? Because their coaches (even the winningest ones) are letting them down.

My daughter has had a love-hate relationship with figure skating for many years. Figure skating is perhaps one of the most stressful sports possible. It reveals the crucible of hope and fear as no other. While other sports allow you nine innings, two halves, three periods, five hundred laps, or at least sixty minutes to do your best, figure skating demands absolute perfection for about three minutes. A single trip or fall, a momentary stumble that would go unnoticed in any other sport, immediately negates a nearly flawless performance.

Sometimes my daughter loves this sport. The music, movement, and grace, and the intimacy and comradeship with other skaters, can motivate her to incredible feats. The truth is that I can watch my son play hockey with mingled anxiety and pleasure, but I simply cannot watch my daughter skate. I cannot watch her leap into the air with razor blades on her feet and no helmet, and I cannot endure watching her fall.

Sometimes my daughter hates this sport. The early mornings, damp arenas, and expense—and the politics, pettiness, and backbiting of skating clubs—can bring her to tears. I find this very frustrating. The very fact that I cannot pick her up when she falls down means that I cannot cheer her up when she is frustrated. She needs a coach—a real coach.

Unfortunately, most figure skating coaches seem merely to function as technical advisors. Their goal is to compete in the Olympics, rather than develop young adults. The ambivalence of figure skating clubs about real coaching is the hidden cause of my daughter's ambivalence about skating. Lauren wants to grow as a person through skating, and if a few medals come her way, so much the better. The coaches want to win medals, and if my daughter grows as a person along the way, it will be a fringe benefit.

Occasionally, a coach might pick my daughter up after a fall and offer comfort and encouragement. More often, a coach will pick her up only to reproach her faulty technique. Coaches rarely help the girls cope with early mornings, damp arenas, and high costs, nor do they help them survive the politics to build healthy lifestyles and relationships. In the glitz and pressure of the figure skating world, too many coaches and clubs fail to realize that truly healthy people are more likely to win those medals than unhealthy people.

This issue of health is the deeper meaning behind the pitching coach's advice to the Blue Jays' Kelvim Escobar. "I was just telling him that in a game like this you've got to go out there and *be ready*," says the coach. But what does it mean to "be ready"? "Readiness" is more than warm-ups and batting practice. It is even more than a state of mind. It is a state of life. Real coaching helps create that state of life.

◆ *Animation:* Truly effective coaches are passionate about the game. Win, lose, or draw, they invest all their emotion and energy into the process. They value the quality of one's performance. They never accept mediocrity. They may coax gently or explode volubly, but they invest everything they have in their players.

◆ *Synergy*: Truly effective coaches synthesize a big picture. They can discern between the aberration of a bad day, and the chronic problem of a bad attitude. They build in themselves and others a quiet confidence and calm. It is an inner harmony that is at once self-satisfied and restless. They may be momentarily irritated or pleased, but they always balance the experience of today with the larger quest.

◆ *Quality relationships:* Truly effective coaches build teams, not just individuals. The inner harmony becomes manifest in practical cooperation and respect. Effective coaches both give and receive advice. They know when to give firm direction and when to build consensus. They may impose discipline or relax the rules, but they always build the morale of the team.

◆ *Personal growth:* Truly effective coaches prioritize personal growth over winning. Skills for working and skills for living are inseparable. The ability of an individual to find fulfillment in daily living, develop balanced self-esteem, and gain clarity of purpose will help one survive the crucible of hope and fear to perform well for the long term.

This is what it means to be ready for the big game, because this is what it means to be ready for life itself. Readiness may be like a coiled spring eager to be released, but once released, it should smoothly accomplish both the task at hand and the fulfillment of its own destiny.

The accomplishment of a task (be it winning a game or implementing a church program) is both related to, and distinct from, the fulfillment of a destiny (be it personal or corporate). The best coaches intuitively realize this. They do not need to be philosophers. They simply understand that victory over competitors and victory over one's self are intrinsically connected. Behind the four keys to effective coaching lies a fifth, and with this we plunge into deeper spiritual waters.

Self-Mastery and Self-Surrender

Good coaches have long recognized the connection between competitive success and personal discipline. Self-mastery is a particularly popular notion with the generation of baby boomers, who may not practice it, but at least value it. Boomers believe in professionalism, and they value competency. Fitness clubs, weight training, jogging, high-protein diets, confidence-building self-help books, and therapy with sports psychologists are all aspects of the quest for self-mastery. One needs to be disciplined in order to win.

The classic advice to *know thyself* has been interpreted in the modern era to mean *control thyself*—or perhaps more specifically to mean *control thy* professional *self.* This modern limitation on self-discipline explains the paradox of disciplined athletes living almost insanely unhealthy lifestyles. Better coaches recognize that self-mastery extends beyond professional competency to personal lifestyle. Daily living, daily intellectual stimulation, daily intimacy, and daily community service—and more—all require the same degree of self-awareness and self-discipline. This more holistic approach to self-mastery is more popular among late-wave boomers. They recognize that one needs to be *healthy*, in the largest sense of that word, in order to win.

The best coaches, however, have also rediscovered the importance of spirituality and healthy living. In the moment of triumph, more and more athletes are seen to pause in the moment of jubilation to kneel in prayer. I make no judgment about the sincerity of such spiritual gestures of humility, but simply point out that this habit is growing. Moreover, gestures of spirituality are as common in times of *defeat* as they are in times of victory, although unseen by the eye of the camera.

The rediscovery of spirituality is particularly important to the "buster" and "echo" generations of the postmodern world. It forces coaches to consider a rather startling paradox. Self-mastery is not enough! Neither professional competency, nor even a disciplined lifestyle, is sufficient to live well. One must seek a connection with the divine.

The difficulty is that coaches may assume that such a

connection is *achievable*. That is, coaches may assume that their role is to help individuals attain it through efforts similar to professional and lifestyle disciplines. Indeed, Christendom generally has encouraged this mistaken assumption, because spirituality has become associated with church attendance, charitable contributions, and proportionate service to ecclesiastical institutions and programs. The best coaches realize that a profound connection with the divine is not *achievable* but only *receivable*. What is needed is not another technique but self-surrender.

Surrender to "the Holy" does not negate the importance of self-mastery. It simply acknowledges a boundary beyond which human effort cannot go. In a sense, this is a key boundary between modernity and postmodernity. It is also a key boundary between the ecclesiastical religion of the twentieth century and the wide-open spiritual quests of the twenty-first century. Encouraging people to perceive, accept, and wrestle with this boundary becomes one of the most challenging tasks of good coaching.

It may seem odd to talk about "sin" and "original sin" in a book about coaching, but it is really unavoidable in the postmodern world. The real point about sin for the postmodern world has to do not with its origins, but with its *inescapability*. In the end, self-mastery alone (whether in professional competence or personal lifestyle) cannot create the wholeness that empowers both the potential for victory and the survival of defeat. The metaphor for sin today is "addiction." This, too, is an inescapable pattern of self-destruction that cannot be broken by even the most intelligent or self-disciplined people. The ground of hope is found only in the intervention of a "higher power."

How does a coach motivate a desire to win without subtly encouraging his or her athletes to abuse steroids? How does a coach instill a passion to compete without subtly encouraging a violent lifestyle? How does a coach rebuild the morale of a defeated team without re-creating an arrogance that will only be shattered again by the next setback? How does a coach allow the team to celebrate victory without dangerous binges and rioting in the streets? Such addictions point toward the unrelenting sin of sports from which there is no escape, unless self-mastery gives way to surrender to the divine.

Lest readers feel I am digressing too far into the world of sports, let me reframe the questions for religious coaches in the postmodern world. How does a coach motivate a desire for church growth without subtly encouraging church members to abuse clever marketing schemes and the almighty dollar? How does a coach instill a passion to compete for the religious attention of the community without subtly encouraging bigotry? How does a coach rebuild the morale of a divided church without creating a spiritual elitism that will only be shattered by the next tragic funeral? How does a coach allow a church to celebrate a successful capital building campaign or mission project without subsequent lethargy and self-satisfied inwardness? These, too, are addictions that point to the unrelenting sin of church life.

Christian coaching in the postmodern world needs to step beyond the boundaries of control established by past Christendom. Openness to mystery, receptivity to the irrational and unexpected, and readiness to be seized, shaken, and stirred by an ultimately unknowable God are not virtues in which Christendom churches normally excel. The "controllable experience of the Holy"—interpreted by denominations, shaped by liturgies, and packaged by church programs—is the essence of Christendom. It relies on the self-mastery of the clergy—their professional competency, impeccable lifestyle, and allegiance to polity.

Not long ago, I participated in an annual conference of

The United Methodist Church. The theme was "leadership." The guest bishop gave a rousing speech telling how professionalism and competency would rescue the credibility of the clergy. She received a standing ovation. The trouble was that all the people standing were over forty-five. They were either builders who respected offices and titles, or boomers who respected professionalism and competency. The few not standing were under forty-five. These busters and echoes had crossed the boundary into the postmodern world. They did not want professionals who could lead individuals and institutions into various forms of self-control and program management. They sought coaches who could help them go further into self-surrender and profound spirituality.

Somewhat later I participated in a "spirituality-fest" sponsored by an American megachurch. The keynote speaker was a legendary football player. Glancing over the crowd of more than a thousand, I saw clearly that the over–forty-five age groups who attended the judicatory meetings were noticeably absent from this event. They were writing letters to the denominational newsletter decrying the shallowness of an athlete's prayer in the end zone and wondering why younger generations would not attend worship with good liturgy and join church committees. The enthusiastic crowd at the event was listening with rapt attention to a player tell of his struggle with, and victory over, addictions to cocaine, fast cars, and prostitutes, through his surrender to God.

It's Not Just About Sports

I am quite aware that "coaching" has so far been solely associated with sports. While this may be the most easily understood entry point into the concept of coaching today, the metaphor of coaching *athletes* is far too limiting. Life is more complex than high-energy beverages and workouts. The principles of good coaching may be the same, but the *nuances* of great coaching are not. In the chaos of generation and culture, nuance is as important as principle. Let me offer three more metaphors for coaching.

- *The Language Tutor:* Mass migration and cultural diversity in the postmodern world have made communication and cultural sensitivity more important—and more complex—than ever. The ability to teach a language involves more than technical advice about grammar, diction, or pronunciation. It involves an appreciation of perspective, attitude, and lifestyle.

  One of the most influential coaches in my life was my high school Spanish teacher. Under his tutelage we not only memorized vocabulary and practiced ordering from restaurant menus, we also studied indigenous history and read regional novels. But our coach took us beyond this. We read indigenous philosophy and theology, visited sites of historic and local community importance, and interacted with both learned and unlearned Spanish-speaking people. We spent hours discussing (in Spanish) the lyrics of the Beatles' hit songs in addition to sampling food, watching plays, and reading newspapers.

  This language tutor broke the boundaries between the modern and postmodern world. He taught us not only to speak Spanish, but also to think like Spaniards. Indeed, he taught us to appreciate even the nuances of Iberian regionalism. He helped us look at the lives of Hispanic Americans, experience the suffering of native Mexicans, articulate the hope of South American revolutionaries, and interpret history through the eyes of Spanish intellectuals. This rather exceeded the goals of our local high school and got our language tutor into occasional conflict with the administration, but it shaped the lives of many students.

- *The Music Teacher:* Music has become the primary method of shaping and identifying generations, minorities, and subcultures in the postmodern world. Everyday speech may have been reduced to a limited cluster of four-letter words and bizarre vocabulary, but music communicates a subtlety of attitude and diversity of perspective that is intricate and profound. Healthy relationships are crucial to life in the post-modern world—and shared music is crucial to healthy relationships.

Another model of coaching in my life was an amateur jazz musician who formed an octet to play old charts that he had collected over the years. We practiced in his kitchen, never performed in public, tolerated every form of experimentalism possible, and had a whale of a good time. Along the way he showed me the intricacies of the baritone saxophone and helped me move beyond *reading* music to *seeing* music, to *feeling* the musical tones. He never got angry, laughed easily, and stopped frequently to comment on the historical precedents and antecedents of any given lyric or riff. He harmonized the octet, bonded the musicians in friendship, and soared with occasional musical genius all at once.

His amateur coaching contrasted rather starkly with the professional teaching of my university orchestra conductor. The conductor was one of the most irascible and unapproachable people I have ever met. He demanded performance and was indifferent to performers. He imposed the metronome slavishly and insisted upon imitation of the "great musicians." He pitted musicians in each section against one another to vie for the first chair. Although occasionally his eyes would glaze in an ecstasy of mystical meaning during a rare perfect performance, he never seemed able to include anyone else in the moment. I wonder why to this day I prefer the jazz saxophone over the classical clarinet.

- *The Midwife:* Health and renewal have become the most fundamental goals of people in all walks of life. People are more aware of being trapped by unhealthy habits, environments, traditions, and institutions than ever before. Since Bill Easum and I introduced the "midwife" metaphor to describe transforming leadership (*Growing Spiritual Redwoods*, Abingdon Press, 1998), the metaphor has received enormous affirmation. People long not only to be reborn, but also to give birth to the positive potential that lies within them.

    The third model of coaching in my life was an associate pastor of the congregation of my youth. He was the most atypical youth minister I have ever known. Quiet, introverted, nonathletic, and prematurely bald, he was gentle, witty, generous with his time, and intellectual. His sense of irony and his ability to penetrate to the heart of a subject touched teenagers and worried veteran church people. He helped others synthesize life. We spent hours (which I am sure he could ill afford due to pressure to be "visiting seniors" or "recruiting dynamic youth groups") talking about abstract philosophy, biblical hermeneutics, conflict resolution, racial prejudice, personal relationships, and *Peanuts* cartoons. I routinely picked the lock on his office to get at his books. He helped me establish my first cell group. One memorable night he found me collapsed in front of the altar weeping over another failed personal, teenage relationship and stayed with me to restore my balance, missing the board meeting going on in the church parlor.

    His coaching did not fit well with the programmatic expertise and professionalism demanded by the congregation and denomination. He did not organize youth rallies and impressive liturgical celebrations; instead, he helped others give birth to their abilities to organize youth rallies and worship celebrations. He helped people discover and release their potential for leadership. More than this, he helped people customize their gifts to suit changing times, supported them when their handcrafted leadership contradicted traditional institutional expectations, and challenged them to move beyond their plateaus of achievement.

These persons are only some examples of a series of tutors, teachers, and midwives who have coached me over the years. Their coaching may or may not have been connected with their professions. The list includes professors in logic, medieval history, New Testament, and Islam; pastors from nontraditional churches; social workers with nontraditional lifestyles; women and men whose actual work took them to biology labs, landscaping sites, and corporate offices—oh yes, and the African American warehouse supervisor who taught me how to use a forklift and quote poetry at truck drivers. He called anyone under forty "young blood," seemed to never leave the warehouse, and treated the time clock with utter disdain.

I have illustrated these three metaphors for coaching with experiences from my own life. This is not because I am particularly proficient in speaking Spanish, playing jazz, or leading churches. It is because the best models for coaching may be found in your own community or life experience. Look into your past and look around your present, and you will begin to see the coaches who help you make life healthy and whole. What is striking is that they are not necessarily lovable people, or the kind of people with whom you would correspond for the rest of your life. They are just people at the right place at the right time with a passion to guide others through the ambiguities of living. They may or may not be conscious of their vocation. They may or may not earn a living from it. The bad news is they are probably *not* closely linked to the Christendom church. The good news is they can be found virtually everywhere else in the postmodern world.

It's Not About Professionalism

It is not that the best coaches cannot be professionals, but that professionalism tends to get in the way of good coaching. All of my examples experienced significant tensions with their own professions in order to fulfill their destiny as coaches. The teacher exceeded the wishes of the school board; the musician was never certified by a school of music; and the youth minister was eventually asked to leave the congregation. Today, the best coaches are apt to say they had to forsake climbing the corporate or denominational ladder to fulfill their destiny.

If you look to sports to describe good coaching, don't look to *professional* sports. Look to *amateur* sports. In the midst of the hundreds of people "coaching" amateur football, baseball, hockey, and soccer teams for the wrong reasons, and doing it badly, you will find a surprising number of women and men over the age of sixteen who do it amazingly well. Talk with them. You will find that they do not coach sports, they coach people; they do not coach to win games, they coach to release human potential; they do not coach physical fitness, they coach fitness for life.

If you look beyond sports to other sectors of society, you will find the best coaches stepping *beyond* professionalism to fulfill their vocation. Recently I encountered the Beacon Group in Evansville, Indiana. This is a nonprofit organization composed of some of the most successful leaders from corporate business, education, and social service, who share common faith assumptions. They have all found "success" in their chosen professions; they have made millions, achieved awards, and risen high in their respective institutions. Nevertheless, none of them could fulfill their vocation as *coaches* within their career paths. They have stepped out of their professions in order to use their expertise in a larger context of guiding others to give birth to their full potential.

This example has many parallels at the turn of the millennium. More and more leaders from all walks of life, and with varying educational background, are finding that they must step outside their professions to fulfill themselves as coaches. They risk the scoffing of their colleagues, as well as potential career advancement. This is just as true for church leaders. Christendom institutions are designed to train and deploy leaders who are good preachers, liturgists, program managers, therapists, and justice advocates. This leadership development strategy works best in an era when choices are clear and the surrounding cultural environment is relatively stable. In such an era, competency is the most fundamental component of leadership, and professionalism is the key to success.

Unfortunately, the millennium has initiated an era when choices are ambiguous and the cultural environment is wildly unpredictable. People living in such a time require coaches, not professionals.

Professionals	"Coaches"
• are schooled, trained, and certified	• are grown, mentored, and accepted
• implement and manage programs	• create environments to birth potentials
• define the paths to success	• explore the alternatives to failure
• are loyal to a strategic plan	• celebrate freedom to change
• encourage self-discipline	• are self-disciplined about being encouraging

Professionals live within history. They remember history so that they can either preserve it or avoid repeating it. Professionals thrive in a continuity of time and space. The more complex time and space become, the more "professional" church leaders need to be. They take continuing education, earn additional seminary degrees, learn new techniques in time management, and hone new skills for communication and advocacy; and they are at a total loss when the continuities of time and space disintegrate into chaos. Coaches, on the other hand, are at home in chaos. It is not that they do not value skills, but that they no longer assume that mere skillfulness will restore health and harmony. They give birth to original ideas and risk unique experiments. They *make* history.

Chapter Two

The Value of Instant Replay

> Coaches have less to learn from history—
> and more to learn from history—than they expect. They are not only learning from history, they are making history.

Consider the great controversies that shaped Christendom through the modern period. These controversies loom large in our modern memories as decisive events that changed the course of history. They include:

- The "unity" of God
- The authority to appoint bishops and rule the church
- The meaning and authority of Scripture
- The relationship between human rights and divine law

At the time, these controversies were viewed by many ordinary people as trivialities amid the larger issues of foreign invasions, famine and plague, freedom of thought, or racial equality, yet these controversies seemed to focus all of the stress of change into a single debate with multiple implications.

Now consider one of the most significant, heatedly debated controversies of the early postmodern period. It has been debated by professionals, noted by world leaders, widely addressed by every media, and argued vehemently in barrooms. It is a debate that has involved people of every race, culture, language, and economic background. It has been as inclusive, and as emotional, as any of the great controversies of Christendom—and generated as many fistfights and fractured as many friendships. I am referring, of course, to the relative value of the "instant replay."

The instant replay is a television coverage technique to instantly play over, and over again, a brief video clip of a sports event that happened faster than the human eye could interpret it. The purpose of the instant replay is to (1) assign responsibility for any possible infraction of the rules and (2) provide data to learn or improve skills. The controversy is about whether instant replay really accomplishes these two goals, or whether it simply delays and needlessly complicates the game. Many will complain that controversy over instant replay is a mere triviality in the midst of more important issues of the day. Some will be insulted that controversy over instant replay should ever be compared to the "more important" debates of Christendom. Both are mistaken.

Controversy over instant replay focuses all the stress of transition to a postmodern world into a single debate that is accessible to the most ordinary person. More than this, the resolution of this controversy will significantly influence the nature and direction of future leaders (or "coaches") of Christian congregations. The underlying issue is profound: *Is there any point to studying history anymore?* Is there really any merit in revisiting, over and over again, a brief "memory clip" recording a historic event that happened faster than social observers at the time could interpret it? Do we really have anything to gain, or does the whole exercise delay and needlessly complicate the game of life?

Church leaders rarely ask these questions, but if you want to coach change in your congregation you had better ask them. Why? Because every member of the congregation is asking these questions. The same people who debate instant replay wonder why the liturgical year, the lectionary, Bible study, and all the big and small traditions of the institutional church are worth all the energy given to them.

So, let's explore the relative value of instant replay.

On the one hand, instant replay is unhelpful!

We have entered an era for which there seem to be few historical precedents. We are truly "making history" in all of the awesome meaning that statement implies. We are making history as a world, as a nation, and as a Christian church. More unsettling, however, is the realization that we are making history as a community, as a local church, as family units, and as individual human beings. We are not just adding another life cycle in a continuous flow of time. The choices we make, or the choices that are thrust upon us, will literally make history, and our lives—and the lives of our children—will never be the same again.

If the changes we are now experiencing were merely another life cycle—some new stage added to childhood, youth, middle age, and retirement—then all we would require to live through it would be a map. Give us a blueprint, a study guide, a program, or a how-to CD-ROM, and we will be all right! Already the stores are full of self-help resources to guide people step-by-step to good living or mere survival. You can learn how to eat better and live longer or build a better bomb shelter and survive the supposedly imminent threat of economic disaster.

Yet the changes we are now experiencing are not merely another life cycle. They do not have adequate historical precedents. We are not just repeating history, fulfilling history, rewriting history, or even learning from history. We are *making history!* The blueprints, guides, and programs will be inadequate. What we need is a coach to guide us through discontinuity. We need people who can help us break the paralysis of fear, risk new ideas with courage, and provide confidence to learn from mistakes.

Consider for a moment what it would feel like to awaken in a place so foreign that not only was the vegetation unfamiliar, but the very laws of nature seemed to have changed. Apples no longer fell down from trees but fell at a twenty degree angle to the ground. Dandelions required song, rather than water, to grow. The sun rose in the east and routinely performed three loops in the sky before setting in the south. All of the ordinary, day-to-day *predictability* of living had vanished. Such a world would be dangerous, but not necessarily fatal. It would be habit, the unthinking repetition of actions based on past predictability, that would be fatal. The mere study and preservation of the past would be deadly. The ability to learn and adapt would be crucial, and the need for contemporary tutors would be paramount.

Christendom churches are now awakening in a world so foreign that not only are the neighborhood and the workplace unfamiliar, but the very laws of spirituality seem to have changed. Sunday morning is no longer a time for restful reflection. People require music, not responsive readings, to grow. Life journeys wander from horizon to horizon and rebound from crisis to crisis before finally setting in a twilight zone somewhere between heaven and hell. All the predictability of life stages and appropriate ecclesiastical interventions has vanished, yet spiritual issues dominate life as never before. It is not the cultural environment that will be fatal to churches, but their habits. The mere replay of cherished historical moments will kill the church. The ability to learn and adapt is crucial, and the need for contemporary mentors is paramount.

On the other hand, instant replay is crucial!

If the replay of selected scenes is unhelpful, the replay of the full-length, unedited movie is very helpful, indeed. It establishes a broader context that we can use to interpret the complexities and ambiguities of human behavior and divine action.

I have long admired Barbara Tuchman's classic study of fourteenth-century Europe, in which she argues that the chaos of the fourteenth and twentieth centuries are profoundly comparable.[1] What exactly was happening in the world while John Wycliffe attacked the papacy and Jan Hus lectured in Prague?[2]

▲   Europe and northern China were being devastated by plague. While peasants revolted in England, the Ottoman Turks conquered the Middle East, Tamerlane invaded India, Acamapitzin became the first Aztec king, and Serbia was lost to the Turks in the battle of Kosovo.

▲   Europe experienced agricultural depression but improved gunpowder and artillery. Meanwhile, India developed the first department of agriculture to combat famine, China invented water-powered machinery to manufacture iron and silk, and Al-Farisi wrote *Correction of the Optics* in which he explained the phenomenon of rainbows.

▲   While Europe lamented the papal schism between Rome and Avignon, Zen Buddhism and Shinto spread in Japan, Islam established itself in the southeast Asian islands, and Timbuktu culture flourished in Africa. The

Greeks were torn between the mystic teach-
ings from Mount Athos and the rationalism of
the Greek Orthodox clergy.

▲   While Gloucester Cathedral built a cloister,
Iberian Arabs built the Alhambra, the Ming
dynasty repaired the Great Wall of China,
Japan built the Golden Pavilion in Kyoto,
Russia built the Cathedral of the Transfigura-
tion in Novgorod, and the Aztecs founded
Tenochtitlán. The Incas introduced Quechua as
the world's first official language.

The point of this comparison of cultures is not the assur-
ance that following today's chaos everything will turn
out just fine, and it is certainly not a guarantee that renaissance is just around the corner. Nor is the point of the
comparison that fourteenth-century solutions can
become twenty-first-century programs. The real point of
the comparison is that *coaching change was all important.*
    During all the confusion and uncertainty of the four-
teenth century, Geoffrey Chaucer wrote *Canterbury Tales*,
William Langland wrote *Piers Plowman*, and Dante
Alighieri wrote *The Divine Comedy.* Li Hsing Tao produced
the play *The Chalk Circle*, the Persian poet Hafiz wrote
Divan, and Meister Eckehart wrote about mysticism and
spirituality. Giotto painted frescoes, Wang Meng established a new Chinese school of art, Guillaume de Machaut
unveiled the "ars nova" style Mass. The redoubtable
world travelers Ibn Khaldun and Ibn Battuta explored
the Sahara and wrote eyewitness accounts of the civilization of Mali. Boccaccio, Petrarch, Gower, Froissart, Wu
Chen, Muto Shui, Al-Farisi, and unknown creative individuals from Venice to Nigeria were all "making history."
    If these coaches of change lived today, then Chaucer,
Dante, Li Hsing, and Ibn Khaldun would all have been
linked by E-mail. The expansion of Mayan trade in

Central America, Muslim trade in southeast Asia, and Mali trade in Africa would have been integrated by overnight courier to the manufacturing centers in China and by electronic financial transfers to the banks in Venice. What might have happened if the department of agriculture in India had advised European governments? Or if Meister Eckehart had visited Japan? Or if Chinese Emperor Hung-wu had negotiated a settlement between Serbs and Turks in Kosovo?

It appears that the value of instant replay does not lie in the selection of video clips from history, thus subject to the ideology and theology of authorities in the media booth or denominational office, but rather it lies in the potential to gain an overview of the whole game. What is crucial is not the repetition of a liturgical year, but the spectrum of human life and divine intervention.

Let's look at the controversy again.

On the one hand, instant replay is unhelpful!

We have entered an era when neither the past nor the present is important. It is the future that is important, and, more significant, the *seeming inevitability* of that future. Instead of helping people learn from their mistakes and do better, instant replay actually reinforces a sense of inevitable doom. The video booth keeps rerunning the same video clips over and over and over again. It never changes. The same actions, the same yearnings, the same attempts, the same sweat, the same expectations, the same cheers or groans from the crowd are repeated. It is as if the lessons of history reinforced the message: *All we can do is the same thing over and over again—only now we can do it with atomic bombs, biological warfare, and genetic engineering. Give up!*

The instant replay has become a vehicle of control. The politicians who quote history, the media that reruns nostalgic documentaries "lest we forget," and, yes, the clergy who insist upon seemingly interminable unison and responsive readings about places and people with names no one can even pronounce anymore are all doing so for the implicit purpose of entrapping people in a box of historical precedent about which the politicians, the media, and the clergy are the experts. Every time a condescending voice quotes, "Those who do not learn from history are condemned to repeat it," the public subsequently discovers that they have been deceived into endorsing the particular ideological or theological agenda of someone else.

The point is that history is a box, and the postmodern public wants to get out of it. The instant replay is unhelpful because it keeps people scrambling around in the box. Many of the same postmodern people who reject instant replay surf the Internet, invent new corporations, discover new ways to feed the poor, and create new art forms. Unfortunately, they also voraciously devour horoscopes, dial 900 to talk to their "psychic friend," and send money to the charismatic religious leader with the best angle on Armageddon.

On the other hand, instant replay is crucial!

If viewing the same event from a hundred different angles from within the same box is unhelpful, viewing life experience with an eye to identifying leverage points for change is helpful, indeed. We can discover hidden possibilities our ancestors missed or which have only emerged today.

If the fourteenth and twentieth centuries are comparable, perhaps comparing the first and twenty-first centuries will be enlightening. The public has been drawn by the passing of the millennium to compare our times with the previous millennial mark of A.D. 1000. Once again, change is anticipated with a shudder of dread and more than a gleam of vengeance. Prophecies of economic chaos, political anarchy, and spiritual judgment abound, filling ordinary, intelligent, generally good people with a natural desire to find something solid and cling to it.

Yet, theologians like Raymond Bulman point out that millennial change, like all change, contains an implicit hope.

> But there is a far more important lesson to be learned from the history of the year 1000. The prediction of disasters, calamities, and global tribulations is never the last word in a genuinely millennial faith. Millennialism is in the long run optimistic. For the persecuted Christians of the first century church, the image of the millennium provided a vision of hope in face of their daily experience of suffering, danger, and desperation. . . . The key to millennial belief is that God is the Lord of History.[3]

The expression of this hope in the year 1000 emerged from the collapse of the Roman Empire and the chaos of the Dark Ages to become a series of "Peace Councils" that brought new stability and renewed moral commitment to Europe.

Nevertheless, the hope of the millennial turn of A.D. 1000 was never about history, but about discerning leverage. Mentors, tutors, spiritual guides—coaches— discovered microscopic methods for macroscopic change. Despite the dire predictions of the end of the world, individuals (some known and many unknown) were "making history":

▲ Stephen I and Boleslaw I were the first kings of Hungary and Poland. Basil II revived Byzantine culture. Leif Ericson sailed across the edge of the world to reach Nova Scotia.

▲ Avicenna wrote his *Canon of Medicine*, Michael Psellus wrote the *Chronographia*, and Murasaki Shikibu wrote

Japanese novels. Chinese painting achieved vivid realism with painters like Kuo Hsi and Ts'ui Po.

▲ Unknown inventors developed the compass and the lateen sail. The Chinese perfected clocks, spinning wheels, paper currency, and movable type printing. The Arabs improved navigational tables and medicine, the Cambodians built hydraulic works for irrigation; the Anasazi built canals, and the first apartment houses were constructed in the American Southwest.[4]

The history they were making helped shape emerging nations and cultures, but more significant, these changes affected the daily living of communities, families, and individuals. Creative, risky, and daring, most of their ideas were likely greeted with skepticism or hostility. No doubt many so-called prophetic voices wondered why they should bother since the end of the world was coming. Nevertheless, these coaches-of-change were the ones to bring hope for the future by identifying the missed leverage points of the past.

So What Is the Advantage to Instant Replay?

Does instant replay help or hinder the flow of the game or the accomplishment of God's mission?

1) *The instant replay assigns responsibility for infractions of the rules.* Postmodern sports enthusiasts, however, have realized that this does not matter in the larger flow of the game. Coaches are occasionally willing to accept blame for something the player did not do, and they are occasionally willing to benefit from something the umpire missed, for the sake of the larger momentum of the game. Fixing blame is secondary. Creating the next original play that will take everyone by surprise is primary. It is useless for a wide receiver in football to blame

interference for his failure to catch the ball; his job is to catch the ball *despite the interference.*

In the same way, postmodern coaches who are enthusiastic for God's mission field do not spend much time fixing blame on others for their team's inability to thrive in mission. The replay of events does not matter. It is not the fault of the government or big business or the local economy, or the insensitive bishop or the out-of-tune piano or the unskilled laity or the crazy clergy. The church cannot shrug off responsibility for its inability to pursue mission by replaying a clip from the past and saying, "The devil made me do it." Interference is embedded in the very nature of the postmodern world. The job of the church is to do God's mission in spite of it.

This is not to say that instant replay is bad. A little common sense has led the football leagues to judiciously allow its use when precision in assigning responsibility is crucial to the game. A little common sense has led church leaders to judiciously allow its use when addressing an abuse is crucial to the mission. The most important advantage, however, is that it has reminded the players that the future is always in *their* hands—not determined by the actions of either the sinners or the saints of the past.

2) *The instant replay provides data to learn or improve skills.* Postmodern sports enthusiasts, however, have realized that they have less to learn—and more to learn—than they expected. There really is not much that they can learn that will *improve skills.* A player may gain a few tips and suggestions, but more often than not, the player will simply do the same thing again, and perhaps the hundreds of interdependent factors that all happen in a split second will result in a catch *this time.* On the other hand, there is a great deal that a player can learn from instant replay that will *improve character.* When everything happens in a split second, spontaneity is crucial. Success will have more to do with identity than skills.

In the same way, postmodern coaches who are enthusiastic for God's mission field have less to learn from history—and more to learn from history—than they expect. They find that they have less to learn from the big names, the pivotal events, and the venerable saints than they thought. Personalities, circumstances, and church context have changed. On the other hand, they find they have much to learn from anonymous, ordinary people, everyday life, and unknown Christians. Hope springs from where you least expect it. It isn't the "big name" players who lead through radical discontinuity and make history—it's the "no name" players who do it.

Living with the Ambiguity of Instant Replay

As churches transition into the postmodern world, church leaders must wrestle with the relative ambiguity of instant replay. They are not just learning from history; they are making history. Survival is not a matter of preservation, but of adaptation. Since God's call is not merely to live but to *abundantly* live, adaptation and change will accelerate even more. Church leaders who would be coaches for change must recognize that history is only *relatively* valuable. It is not worthless and cannot be discarded. Its worth, however, is measured differently. It is not the simplicity of history that is crucial, but its complexity. It is not the predictability within history that is cherished, but the chaos.

Radical Imagination
The first response to living in a time of making history is "wild" creativity. Coaches wrestling with the relative ambiguity of instant replay imaginatively create new laws to govern their behavior. In sports, they invent new rules, create original plays, model new moves, and redefine the positions on a team. In life, they create fantasy worlds, alternate universes, and fictional

realities to help them make sense of their lives. More important, these fantasies are used to restructure daily living and import a hitherto foreign pattern for behavior. The resurgence of fantasy can be seen throughout postmodern culture.

▲ The abundance of books in the fantasy and science fiction genres
▲ The popularity of futuristic or post-Armageddon adventure movies
▲ The prime time marketability of television fantasies about legendary or invented heroes
▲ The media's preoccupation with the supernatural, the magical, or the bizarre
▲ The explosion of interactive CD-ROM games that allow participants to alter historic events, create new worlds, and write their own rules of behavior

Postmodern imagination is filled with spiritual speculation. Often accused of historical inaccuracy, critics of postmodernism do not understand that what is a failing for the modern world is a virtue for making history. In the new era, creativity is more important than memory, because old habits are no longer effective to survive daily living.

The power of radical imagination is not merely that people create an alternative reality, but that people seek to import new laws of predictable behavior into their own daily living. Postmodern people are creating a new matrix of behavioral expectations based on unique worldviews. They behave at work, at home, at play, and on the highway as if the laws of their fantasy were true. At its most extreme, this can be dangerous. There is more than one story in every small town and urban center about violence, psychological imbalance, or family conflict due to the incompatibility between fantasy and daily living. The power of imagination to break down barriers and resolve disputes, on the other hand, invents solutions and "draws outside the lines" of conventional wisdom. Radical imagination in a time of making history is reshaping the economics, politics, technologies, and philosophies of daily life.

Imagination is also changing the experience and celebration of God. Religion is being redefined in unexpected ways. There is a "fanatical fringe" including such religious expressions as the Order of the Solar Temple, Heaven's Gate, and the Branch Davidians; doomsday preachers and apocalyptic writers; visions of rapture, visions of UFOs, and visions of Mary.[5] Beyond the fanatical minority, however, there is an enormous movement of creative Christianity redefining the life of the church.

- Congregational worship is importing the images, sounds, movement, and light of surrounding culture through multiple, interactive media and exploring the mutual relevance of the gospel and daily living.
- Congregational organization is adapting the methodologies of cells, organisms, and entrepreneurship and discovering new paths to spiritual growth and accelerated mission.
- Congregational mission is forming new partnerships with agencies and organizations crossing public sectors and faith boundaries, and it is addressing issues of health, economics, environment, and peace.

In a complete reversal of the hierarchical world of the previous two millennia, the more localized change is, the more imaginative experiments become. Standardization has given way to contextualization. The people who are really making history today are not the elite few in government, corporate, or university positions; but they are indigenous community and church leaders. Perhaps never before have ordinary people—and local churches—had such power to make history.

Obsessive Timidity

The second response to living in a time of making history is a form of immobility. It is not the paralysis of a deer caught on a dark night in the beam of a car's headlights; it is the frantic activity of a mouse running through a maze. The only escape is to leap over the walls of the maze, but the mouse chooses instead to rush round and round the familiar corridors of its world rather than fling itself into the unknown. A more intelligent mouse might even disassemble the corridor walls and restructure the maze in a vain effort to make its habitat truly livable. In the end, the mouse just frantically races around the newly renovated space and never seems to get anywhere.

Despite the radical imagination changing the face of church life, such obsessive timidity is commonly seen among congregations and denominations caught in the maze of Christendom. It is not a fear of change, so much as the fear of losing control of change. Traditional Christendom congregational and denominational structures prioritize the preservation of history, not the making of history. When precedent becomes more important than imagination in an age of global discontinuities, church structures marginalize themselves.

- Board decision making becomes preoccupied with ever smaller trivialities.
- Denominational structures dither about political correctness.
- Middle judicatories are sidetracked in litigation and capital development for maintenance.
- Church leaders ignore demographic research.
- Church structures respond slowly and inadequately to technological change.
- Leadership recruitment is strangled by outmoded credentialing policies.

- Leadership training is bottlenecked by tenure tracks and core curricula.
- Leadership deployment is delayed by the protection of entitlements and seniority.
- Worship planners argue endlessly over the method for distributing the sacraments.
- Sunday school teachers search fruitlessly for the perfect curriculum.

It is not culture that has left the church stranded on an island of Sunday mornings; it is the church that has chosen to maroon itself.

Ironically, the same congregational leaders who demonstrate (or tolerate) remarkable imagination working with social agencies, businesses, and governments become obsessively timid in the church.

> "Everything else in my life is changing," complains a member of the board, "but the one unchanging rock in my existence will be the church!"

> "We can't do that!" exclaims the denominational committee. "It isn't part of our ethos!"

The church becomes an anchor restraining effective mission rather than a leader in innovative mission. It resists upgrading technology, adapting new organizational models, developing new marketing skills, modernizing property, or cooperating with other partners in mission, not because this is unaffordable or impractical, but because it symbolically acknowledges the importance of change itself.

Obsessive timidity is also a reaction of the government, social service, and corporate sectors to a time of making history. The inability of national coalitions to resolve ethnic disputes or intervene in global disasters is also a sign of the fear of losing control over change. One might argue that the ineffectiveness of health care systems to provide equal accessibility to the public is a sign that the structures can no longer keep pace with their own medical advances. Chronic crises in public education reflect the preoccupation of community members with internal politics rather than with changing community dynamics. Bankruptcy and merger, boom and bust, and the volatility of the stock market reflect the agony of businesses trying to find a place in a postcapitalist world—brought about by postmodernism—in which land, labor, and cash have become secondary to information, knowledge, and technology.

Living Between Imagination and Timidity

Many people reading a history of the first century will be impressed by the seeming chaos of religion and culture. Radical imagination and obsessive timidity not only clash, but they also become bound together in every achievement or disaster. Whenever there is an exciting breakthrough to celebrate, it is accompanied by a darker potential. Whenever there is a tragic development, it is accompanied by a brighter hope. This cycle is seen not only during the first century but throughout history.

▲ Movable-type printing enables the dissemination of ideas to liberate the mind—or subvert faith.
▲ The invention of gunpowder enables the control of behavior—or liberation from injustice.
▲ The first compasses allow travelers to explore the world—or exploit other nations.

Radical imagination revolutionizes Christian worship with the invention of sight-singing by Guido d'Arezzo. At the same time, heretics are burned in Orleans. Westminster Abbey and the White Tower of London are both erected in the same era within trumpet distance of each other, and subsequently, it will not always be clear which is a force of good and which is a force of evil. The spiritual ferment of the times births both original spiritual movements and authoritarian religious institutions. If the first century birthed new orders of Carthusians and Cistercians, and revived religions like the cult of Gautama Buddha (Japan), the cult of Siva (India), and the religious experiences intended by the Toltec temple of Chichén Itzà and the platform mounds of the Mississippi Valley, then what strange diversity of spirituality will be birthed by the spiritual ferment of the twenty-first century?

What does it mean to live between radical imagination and obsessive timidity? It means that *irony* will replace *solemnity* as the normative principle of human behavior. The more serious the human condition becomes, the less seriously it is treated. The grim countenance and serious determination of Christian true believers are being replaced by a hearty and irreverent sense of humor. In the twentieth century, the complexity of life caused people to work harder. In the twenty-first century, the ambiguity of life causes people to laugh harder. It is the only way to endure it and, eventually, triumph over it.

It means that *apocalyptic* will replace *ethics* as the cornerstone of religious conversation. The more entrapping the human condition becomes, the less likely liberation will be accomplished by human achievement. The political savvy and moral certitude of Christian advocates for social change is replaced by a hearty and irrational sense of hope. In the twentieth century, the injustice of life caused people to redesign the social order. In the twenty-first century, the entrapment of life causes people to long for Eden.

It means that *identity* will replace *planning* as the key to building enduring organizations. The more chaotic the human condition becomes, the less strategically it can be organized. The tactical expertise and transferable blue-prints of church growth specialists is being replaced by a clearly and aggressively articulated congregational identity. In the twentieth century, the reliability of social and ecclesiastical safety nets caused people to design five-year plans and three-year budgeting cycles. In the twenty-first century, the unpredictability of life causes people to identify boundaries defined by clear consensus about core values, beliefs, vision, and mission.

In the emerging ambiguity around instant replay, Christian coaches laugh readily, look for the unexpected, and emphasize and embed identity. The old polarities of "left" and "right," "evangelical" and "mainstream," "charismatic" and "fundamentalist," "protestant" and "catholic" are melting down in the crucible of ironic living. It is as if Moses, Mary, and Monty Python had formed a global alliance.

Notes

1. Barbara Tuchman, *A Distant Mirror: The Calamitous 14th Century* (New York: Knopf, 1978).
2. See *The Atlas of Medieval Man* by Colin Platt (New York: St. Martin's Press, 1979), p. 192.
3. Raymond Bulman, *The Lure of the Millennium* (Maryknoll, New York: Orbis Books, 1999), p. 16.
4. *The Atlas of Medieval Man*, pp. 52-53.
5. *The Lure of the Millennium*, pp. 47-61.

Chapter Three

Coaching Teams

> The postmodern church is a gathering of good people who want to work together to be a blessing to humankind. These teams do not need a guardian, a CEO, or a caregiver. They need a coach.

The most demanding test for spiritual leadership in the twenty-first century is the ability to motivate twenty twelve-year-old boys to play ice hockey at 5:30 on a Saturday morning in mid-January and have fun. I am not just being fanciful. How many Chris-tendom clergy could accomplish the following feat of leadership displayed by the amateur coaches of my son's ice hockey team?

At 5:30 A.M. my son *willingly* and *without coaxing* got up, bolted breakfast, drove with me to a cold arena, and laboriously donned strange and bulky gear in order to exhaust himself chasing a puck around a slippery ice rink while being repeatedly checked, tripped, and harassed by other players (some of whom were from his own team). Why would he do this?

The coach arrived at the rink by 5:00 A.M., welcomed the boys with alert enthusiasm, and joined them in the locker room. He laced their skates, taped their sticks, laughed at their jokes, and answered their questions amid a steady stream of tips customized for every player by name. He reviewed the strategy, reminded them of the rules, and pushed them to do their pre-game stretches. He encouraged the good players, reinforced the bad players, and woke up the sleepy players. Upon discovering that the goalie had overslept, he laughed instead of cursed, called him without making him feel guilty, and waited for him at the door. He insisted on fair play, called every legitimate penalty, celebrated every goal, lamented every shot off the crossbar.

After the game was over and the team had lost 15 to 6, he reviewed the play, gave them all a pep talk, and invited them to the team party the next day. When one boy was practically in tears having missed nine (count them, *nine*) opportunities to score, he sat another half hour in the cold arena helping the boy understand the difference between self-criticism and self-hatred, bought him hot chocolate, and sent him home ready to get up at 5:30 A.M. the next week to do it all over again.

The same coach spent another two hours with his assistants during the week training them to do the same things. He made a mental note on this particular morning to speculate with his assistant coach about the possibility that *that* boy might become captain of the team.

Now, translate that into church experience. How many church members *willingly* and *without coaxing* get up every morning to go into the cold, inhospitable world to pursue Christ's mission while being continually checked, tripped, and harassed by others (including, God bless them, some of their own fellow church members who have not learned to get out of the way). And how many church leaders can help them do it continually, watch them fail frequently, teach them the difference between self-criticism and self-hatred, and help them discover and deliver their full potential as servants of God?

The most essential requirement to be a coach is to have a team. That is also the most overlooked truth in church leadership. Recently, I attended a conference of university and seminary teachers. During the Saturday afternoon break, many were gathered in the hotel lounge around wide-screen televisions watching a key football game between Michigan State and Notre Dame. The rivalry was intense, and the game was close. The watchers shouted criticism and encouragement at the television. One person in particular ranted about the quality of coaching for one of the teams. He was not only loud, but he was also remarkably articulate. He clearly knew the game. He understood the theory of the game, he had a broad knowledge of the tactics of the game, and he genuinely loved the game. He brought the full analytical power of his university professorship to bear on the game. Only one crucial thing was missing. An exasperated waiter who could not hear the game because of the ranting pointed it out. He said: *If you're such a great coach, then where is your team?*

The difference between an armchair coach and a real coach is that the latter actually has a team. Coach and team go together. One can imagine a prophet without listeners, a priest without worshipers, and even a teacher without students, but one cannot imagine a coach without a team. To be a coach is to eat, sleep, work, play, move, travel, and live with teams. You are behind the bench with a team, on the bus with a team, at breakfast with a team, in the hotel room with the team, and yes, even in the showers with the team. You are not sitting in an armchair, working in a private study, taking a solitary day off, or traveling by a separate route. Coach and team are inseparable. If you think you are a coach, but you do not have a team, then you are not really a coach. In fact, you're not even in the game.

Coaching has not been a pastoral leadership role for the traditional church. Traditionally, the church has separated leaders from followers, clergy from laity, and CEOs from committees. Church leaders have been authorities and experts who were too preoccupied with private studies, a solitary day off, or traveling by a separate continuing education allowance. Consider a common congregational dilemma like the need to initiate a new outreach mission: How will we do it?

▲ The premodern answer: *Let's get an authority from the home office to tell us how to do it!*
▲ The modern answer: *Let's hire a professional to do it for us!*
▲ The postmodern answer: *Let's build a team and turn them loose!*

In sports metaphors, traditional church leadership has behaved more like an owner than a coach. Church leaders tell people what to do, and then do "chief executive officer stuff" in the owner's box. In more recent decades, church leadership behaves more like a highly paid player. The team watches from the pews in the dugout, while leadership hits all the home runs. In the last gasp of Christendom, church leadership even behaves like the cheerleaders. It does amazing leaps, stirs up the crowd, and sings the school song—caring little whether the team is actually winning or losing on the playing field. Traditional church leadership may behave like an owner, a player, or a cheerleader—but not like a coach.

Coaching is a postmodern leadership role, and tradi-tionally trained clergy and veteran laity are not familiar with it. This is a unity of leader and follower that is so intimate that the distinction between who is leading and who is following at any given moment is impossible to make. The coach and the team share everything—the bruises, the sleepless nights, the burden of travel, the joy of victory, the crush of defeat, and the courage to try again. There is no team without a coach, and there is no coach without a team. The hierarchies and bureaucracies of Christendom insisted on some form of elitism. A few led—because they held an office, were certified by a denomination, were more knowledgeable, more pure, more correct, more spiritual, or simply paid to do it—and everybody else dutifully followed. In the postmod-ern world, everybody on the team is a leader, and every-body on the team is a follower, and the coach helps each player discern when to be one or the other. Coach and team are distinct, yet inseparable. Let's look at both sides of this dynamic, essential relationship.

The Coach

A great coach brings to the team more than expertise, much more than personality, and far more than the con-fidence of the team owner. A great coach brings to the team four things:

- ✔ a mission attitude
- ✔ a work ethic
- ✔ a variable game plan
- ✔ a winning faith

These four characteristics build quality teams. One can apply the same attributes to sports, business, music, and any corporate endeavor in the postmodern world. Here I simply apply them to churches.

A Mission Attitude

Attitude implies a specific posture toward the world. It is not a psychological quirk or an aggressive or passive demeanor; it is a predictable manner of behaving in daily life. It goes beyond the professionalism of traditional church leadership and is manifest in the smallest details of living. The world probably views this attitude as eccentric because it seems arrogant at precisely the times the world expects modesty, and it is modest at precisely the times the world expects self-aggrandizement. Coaches are "on a mission." Their single-mindedness makes them link personal identity to the mission, so they seem arrogant. Yet when mission goals are accomplished, their personality fades into the background. There are seven signs of an authentic mission attitude:

1. *Clarity.* Coaches with a mission attitude are remarkably sure of their own core values and beliefs. They have spent long hours alone and in partnerships with an extraordinary variety of people exploring what they are prepared to die for. They know the boundaries that they will not go beyond, the assumptions that will be transparent in their lifestyles, and the bedrock faith to which they will return again and again for strength in the midst of adversity. They know the mistakes they habitually make and strive to correct. They know the shame of sin and the iron resolve to be true to God-given potential.

2. *Humility.* Coaches with a mission attitude are remarkably flexible. Like the medieval church leaders of old, they can play many different roles and relate to many different cultures. They never tie themselves to one job, one task, or one personality. At one moment they can be warm and kind, and at another moment they can be cold and challenging. They give the same attention to small details as they do to turning point

decisions. Why? Because they never know when that small detail will become the hidden turning point in the life of an individual or a church. *They do not know.* They know that they do not know, and they act accordingly.

3. *Passion.* Coaches with a mission attitude make a total emotional commitment to a vision of change. They hold nothing back. They are committed to their own mental, relational, and physical health, not as ends in themselves, but as necessary means to pursue their vision. They are excited to talk about the mission, restless to accomplish mission, eager to celebrate mission, and thrilled to share mission with partners. Postmodern coaches do not love the church; they love the mission. Nothing will be allowed to get in the way of the mission, not even the institutional church.

4. *Urgency.* Coaches with a mission attitude are impatient. They take time to think and plan, but they do not have time to dither. Decisions will not be put off until after the busy Advent season or until people have rested from the recent turkey supper. They know that postmodern culture is racing to outdistance the church at lightning speed and that Christ is with postmodern people, not sitting idly at the turkey supper. They are determined to carry the mission of Jesus to the point of human need as quickly and effectively as possible. That is why they are prepared to jettison any and all excess baggage to get there.

5. *Curiosity.* Coaches with a mission attitude always feel inadequate. Therefore, they are always learning and growing. Every mystery intrigues them. Every unique personality, every unexpected cultural event, every odd experience is pregnant with potential insight. They ask questions constantly, filing away

miscellaneous information. They are constantly revising their thinking in light of new discoveries. They are always searching for another door, a new vehicle of communication, or a hitherto hidden opportunity with which to bring the gospel to bear on the predicaments of human life.

6. *Caring.* Coaches with a mission attitude prioritize relationships within the team and beyond it. Their primary compassion is for the lost person. They care most for the broken, the hungry, the seeking, the aimless, the addicted, and the victimized public who could experience immeasurable benefit if they entered into a relationship with Christ. They care for the church insider, the institutional church veteran, and the church member, but only as potential leaders pregnant with the possibilities of God. Their caring may not help people die with dignity, but it will help people live abundantly.

7. *Joy.* Coaches with a mission attitude live in harmony with their destiny. That is why they have serenity or calm in the midst of the chaos surrounding them. They are not distracted by the agendas of other people. They are not sidetracked by a committee that is irrelevant to the mission they are pursuing. They are aware of their calling, vocation, or purpose in life. The vision that has captured their heart is like a compass setting for their lifestyle and livelihood. They have synchronized their activities with a larger destiny. They find self-fulfillment in self-surrender. That is joy.

The coach brings a mission attitude to the team. He or she lives it and models it. The coach focuses the church beyond itself—beyond its friendliness, property, heritage, program, and good feelings—to prioritize the mission field.

A Work Ethic

A work ethic implies a specific behavior in the world. It is a discipline before which everything else is secondary. It is not an addiction (workaholism), but a methodology for self-fulfillment. The paradox of the modern church is that it generates workaholic clergy and laity who rapidly burn out and remarkable laziness among the membership who cannot maintain even the slightest discipline regarding regular worship or adult spiritual growth. The postmodern church establishes a true work ethic that is healthy and challenging for all. There are concrete expectations about spiritual growth and participatory mission for the membership that go far beyond mere financial contributions and institutional administration.

1. *Gifts discernment.* Coaches with a work ethic help every member of the team discover their spiritual gifts—the inner mission potentialities with which God has created every human being, the exercise of which brings personal fulfillment. Coaches do not fill committee vacancies with dutiful people, but they train individuals to build mission around their gifts.

2. *Skills development.* Coaches with a work ethic motivate team members toward continuous learning. New skills required by the changing mission field are acquired; old skills are perfected. Postmodern churches have large continuing education budgets for volunteers and readily send volunteers out, or bring trainers in, to train leaders for excellence.

3. *Testing.* Coaches with a work ethic encourage team members to take risks, experiment with creative ideas, and carefully evaluate the results. Failure is a God-given opportunity to reevaluate and do better in the future. Participants in the postmodern church are

always testing themselves, pushing the limits, pondering the impossible, and finding a better way.

4. *Persistence*. Coaches with a work ethic are known for their dogged perseverance, not their magnetic personalities. They are nothing if not tenacious about mission. They are patient with experiments, yet they are able to surrender even the most sacred tactic in favor of a better one in order to advance God's mission on earth. They never give up and are always looking for another way.

The coach brings rigor to the team. Faith is a gift, but mission requires hard work. Chaplains may help people wait to enter heaven, taskmasters may help people earn their way into heaven, but coaches help joyous volunteers tear down the dikes of self-interest and dig new canals of self-fulfillment so that heaven can spill over into the world.

A Variable Game Plan

A game plan is a strategy to positively engage the world with Christ. Since the postmodern world is changing every minute, the plan is evolving every second. The modern church either repeated the same tactics over and over again through the liturgical year in sacred monotony or constructed elaborate multistep strategic plans that assumed the world would hold still long enough for them to be effective. The postmodern church does neither. Their coaches design a fresh game plan every week just as sports coaches revise the playbook for every game.

1. *Listening*. Coaches with a variable game plan constantly listen, observe, and interpret the revolutionary changes transforming the mission field every day. They read eclectically, converse with strangers and

enemies, utilize all media, cross all professional disciplines and public sectors, and surf the Internet. They
pray constantly, read scripture daily, and observe
Christ as a third party to every conversation.

2. *Leverage.* Coaches with a variable game plan are
   always looking to maximize the impact of even the
   smallest Christian actions. They focus the limited
   energies of the church wherever it can influence
   events most with Christian values and beliefs. They
   never try to do everything at once. They do a limited,
   but constantly evolving, number of things well.

3. *Opportunism.* Coaches with a variable game plan
   unhesitatingly scrap the best-laid strategic plans to
   seize unexpected opportunities. They take advantage
   of an individual's spiritual breakthrough, a sudden
   shift in cultural context, a surprising invitation from a
   hitherto unknown partner, or any revolutionary
   change to find a way to advance the mission.

4. *Partnership.* Coaches with a variable game plan
   always partner volunteers in mission. It is a spiritual
   platooning in which several players share a strategic
   position on the team. Partners can opportunistically
   use the gifts received from the personal support of the
   partnership. They learn together, support one
   another, and accomplish mission as one.

The coach brings direction and coordination to the team.
The modern church understands this to be administration and diverts the coach into the position of general
manager. The postmodern church understands this to be
spiritual leadership, which is more art than science. It is a
sensitivity to the movement of the Holy Spirit in individual lives and contemporary culture combined with creativity and courage to seize the right moment.

A Winning Faith

A winning faith is a sustaining confidence in the self-understanding of the coach and the team. It is a matter not of achievement but of identity. A winning faith is not the confidence that the team can or will win, but the belief that the team are winners. Whether they win or lose, they are still winners. Such confidence grows within a great coach and inspires the whole team. In a sports team, they believe themselves already to be winners. They play like winners. They take risks like winners. They win like winners. They even lose like winners. They do not need to win to prove to themselves that they are winners. Their identity as winners simply seeks fulfillment in every game they play.

In the postmodern church, a winning faith is a sustaining confidence in redemption. Coach and team do not compete against other churches and organizations, nor do they see their vindication in the outcome of some cosmic struggle against evil. They do not need to achieve anything to prove them worthy. The coach's vindication lies in self-fulfillment in every activity or mission. A winning faith is what you are, not what you hope to do. Coaches who model a winning faith demonstrate four qualities:

1. *Long-term relationship.* Coaches with a winning faith stay with the team through all the ups and downs of congregational life. They have long-term pastoral leadership. Achievements, or the lack of achievements, do not generate prideful complacency or deflated despair. Their identity is grounded in the confidence in their own vocation and their ultimate acceptance by Christ.

2. *Tolerance of errors.* Coaches with a winning faith show remarkable tolerance for the errors, foibles, and mistakes of the team members. Error is evidence of

passion and opportunity to learn. Mistakes reveal the next steps in the quest for quality, but they do not undermine the intrinsic identity of the team as winners.

3. *Uncompromising about growth.* Coaches with a winning faith insist on constant growth for every team member. They are perfectionists in the sense that they are not satisfied unless every team member is playing to his or her fullest potential—and since that potential is unlimited, the coach is never satisfied. They drive themselves and the team in continuous learning and discovery.

4. *Desire for God.* Coaches with a winning faith find their self-fulfillment in their relationship to God, not in the achievement of any short-term goal. They yearn to shape their life, lifestyle, and livelihood around that relationship. They unite the readiness to surrender all for a loving God (agape love) with the deeply emotional desire to immerse themselves in a beloved God (erotikos love). They do not merely believe in God. They want to experience the divine.

Coaches are often perceived as too stubborn, too accommodating, too arrogant, or too self-absorbed by traditional Christendom congregations. This is because the traditional congregation does not understand itself as a team. If they were merely an institution, a social service, a club, or an historical society, they would have no need for a coach. A CEO, a manager, an activities director, or a guardian would do. Once the congregation understands itself to be a team playing on the turf of God's contemporary mission field in order to win a victory for the world over sin and death, the leadership traits of the coach become crucial.

Great coaching was revealed in the 1999 league play-off between the New York Mets and the Atlanta Braves. The Mets' wild card hopes had been a roller coaster ride that season, and only a last-minute winning streak earned them the wild card. They had lost the first three games against Atlanta in the play-offs and were once again on the verge of elimination. Then they won the fourth game—barely. The fifth game was played in pouring rain in New York City and proved to be the longest game in baseball history. The fans cheered throughout the downpour, holding up signs that read *Find a Way!* The camera rarely left Mets coach Bobby Valentine for long periods of time.

- He personified a mission attitude throughout the long game. He was focused, flexible, passionate, restless, questioning, and calm. More than once he stunned the crowd and television commentators by a daring pitching decision, heedless of the jeers or doubts of observers.

- He established a rigorous work ethic. Throughout the long game, he pushed every player to his limit (but never beyond). When base runners were left stranded and hitters threw their bats in frustration, he never wasted time on recrimination or false comfort but set them practicing for the next inning. He used every gift of every player on the team.

- He deployed a flexible game plan. He created his plan, revised it, and ultimately discarded it for a new one. Several times he sent a batter to the plate, recalled him, and changed batters after discerning a hitherto unseen opportunity.

- He had a winning faith. Three times his ace bunter failed to advance runners to break the tie. After fifteen innings and six hours of baseball, Atlanta scored two runs, and it looked as if the game would be over in three more outs. The players wore misery on their faces. Only Valentine's winning faith kept them going. With the bases loaded and two outs, he sent an injured player, who had not performed well for the whole series, to the plate. That player hit a grand-slam home run and won the game.

  The fans cheered, and the entire Mets team ran onto the field. The grand-slam hitter was not even able to touch all the bases. He said he didn't care; he just wanted to get into the clubhouse to celebrate with the team. Meanwhile, Valentine quietly shook hands with his pitching coach and walked to the exit. The camera caught him again. There were tears in his eyes as he looked up at the fans and mouthed the words Thank you, New York! Sports fans know that the Mets finally lost in the sixth game and never reached the World Series. Somehow, that doesn't matter. The real victory had been won—so watch out next year!

The Team

When pastors look at congregations, what exactly do they see? How do they perceive the congregation as a whole? What is the paradigm or filter through which they interpret all the activity of congregational life?

▲ The premodern answer: *Here are sinful people in need of proper guidance.*
▲ The modern answer: *Here are good programs in need of competent administration.*

▲ The postmodern answer: *Here are God's people who yearn to fulfill their destinies.*

The premodern paradigm requires a guardian, an educator, a shepherd. and an occasional prophet. The modern paradigm requires a teacher, an administrator, a chief executive officer, and an occasional priest. The postmodern paradigm requires a coach. When postmodern leaders look at the congregation, they do not see a morass of sin or a collection of programs and committees; they see a gathering of good people who want to work together to be a blessing to humankind. They are a team or, perhaps more accurately, a league of teams. These teams do not need a guardian, a CEO, or a caregiver. They need a coach.

In previous books (*Kicking Habits* [Abingdon Press, 1997] and *Moving Off the Map* [Abingdon Press, 1998]), I have used the following diagram to illustrate what it means to be a team in the Christian church.

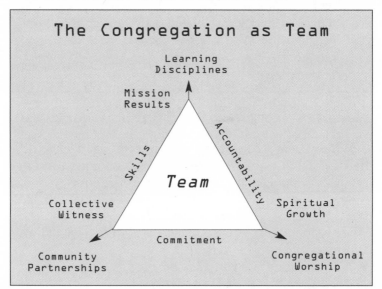

In a sense, this diagram represents the agenda of the Christian coach in the postmodern church. This is what the coach does every day, every week, every year in long-term relationship to the body of Christ. In order for a congregation to be an effective team in the contemporary mission field, they must order their lives around three essential orientations:

Orientation #1: **Three foundations of effective teams**

☆ *Commitment.* This is wholehearted enthusiasm to fulfill the purpose of God to rescue, redeem, and restore all creation to the original perfection of Eden. It is reckless abandonment to the big, audacious, seemingly impossible goal of making God's love real. Like any winning sports team (or any great musical ensemble or any successful organization), the members of the team are so committed to the goal they willingly alter their lifestyles (relationships, diets, exercise and leisure, work habits, and career paths) to stay fit and focused on the accomplishment of the goal.

☆ *Skills development.* This is the priority for every member of the team to recognize and nurture their spiritual gifts, acquire and develop the relevant skills that utilize those gifts, and interface their unique gifts and honed skills with those of others in the team. A shortstop on a baseball team, gifted with mobility and an accurate throwing arm, hones those skills to a fine edge and interfaces that ability with outfielders, first basemen, and catchers. Congregational teams prioritize energy and budget to train every member of the church in what he or she does best.

☆ *Accountability.* This is the peer support and evaluation that constantly tests the degree of commitment and level of skills development against the standard of excellence expected by the entire team. Team members look not to the franchise owner for approval or disapproval but to one another. It is the affirmation of their teammates that they covet, and the approval of a distant denominational office is of little consequence. Such accountability is not accomplished in an annual performance review. It happens every time team members make eye contact.

A true team is an entrepreneurial unit. It is not just a committee by another name. Committees implement someone else's agenda. Committees recruit people to devise and implement strategies to accomplish the purposes of a board, a denomination, or a clergy staff, but they look to someone else to approve that strategy and evaluate their success. Every committee has several redundant layers of management supervising them constantly.

True teams, however, have real power. They have the power to discern, design, implement, and evaluate mission without asking permission from anybody else. This trusted independence allows them to seize unpredicted opportunities instantaneously in the chaos of the postmodern world.

Orientation #2: Three targets of effective teams

☆ *Mission results.* The congregation as a team aims at results, not processes. Their primary concern is not how many or how few are involved. They take no pride in large budgets or small expenses. They care only that individual, community, and global lives have been changed by the person and work of Jesus. Results are what count. Survival means nothing, even if accompanied with harmony and good feeling.

☆ *Collective witness.* The congregation as a team aims at both witness and action. They never take any action without simultaneously sharing the faith motivation behind it. They never share faith without simultaneously doing something of practical benefit for another human being. The tactics of witness may vary with the skills and personalities of the team members. The demand to witness will always be present.

☆ *Spiritual growth.* The congregation as a team aims at spiritual growth. It is not optional; it is required with membership. It does not begin or end at meetings, but it intentionally pervades all church experiences. It is not done by children and appreciated by adults, but done by adults and emulated by children. It is pursued individually and together. It is free to explore any new direction of thought or awareness, and it is relentless.

A true team is an organic cell. It is not just a bureaucratic agency by another name. Committees worry about procedure, separate the deed (which they do) from the rationale of the deed (which somebody else does), accomplish a task, and quit. True teams never stop growing. The depth of their mutual support motivates the richness of their personal and interpersonal growth. The mission is a flowering of the rooted spiritual growth of the organism. Like a climbing rose crossing barbed wire, the beautifying task and the beautiful identity are all one.

Orientation #3: **Three networks of effective teams**

☆ *Learning disciplines.* Congregations, as effective teams, link themselves to networks of relevant learning. Since they are driven by results, they take every opportunity to learn new techniques, technologies, methods, possibilities, and leverage points. No single tactic is sacred. Therefore, the congregation as a team will renovate, relocate, retrain, reinvent, retool, rewire, and reconstruct anything if it will accomplish their goal better.

☆ *Community partnerships.* Congregations, as effective teams, link themselves beyond the church (and denomination). They do not expect all of the gifts and skills required for the contemporary mission field to be present within their membership and do not hesitate to partner with other agencies, organizations, religious groups, or businesses to combine resources to accomplish their goal. Cooperation with culture is not a shameful necessity, but a positive opportunity.

☆ *Congregational worship.* Congregations, as effective teams, build all work, witness, and growth around worship. The need to motivate energy, focus commitment, and prioritize eye-to-eye accountability actually makes worship more important than ever before. Worship fires the desires of God's people. It is the moment before the team runs out onto the playing field when they hold hands, pray, and shout their vision. The routine of passing the peace has nothing to do with friendly greetings and personal introductions. It is the regular opportunity to look your teammate in the eye and ask, "Sister, how is it with thy soul?"

A true team is a holy link between worship and community. It is not just middle management by another name. Committees link programs to boards. Committee members will implement a program precisely—without ever befriending the people who supposedly benefit from it. Committee members never miss a meeting and unfailingly report to the board, but they are remarkably lackadaisical about regular worship participation.

True teams do not need to attend board meetings, but they never fail to participate in a worship experience. The touch of the holy motivates their spiritual growth and prompts them to connect with the real people of God's mission field. They do not need to meet. They need to worship. They do not desire to implement programs. They desire to partner with people.

This is a team: an entrepreneurial unit, an organic cell, a link in the chain of life between God and community. A team requires a coach with a mission attitude, a work ethic, a variable game plan, and a winning faith. The one requires the other. If all you have is committees, all you need is a CEO; and if all you have is a CEO, then all you need is committees. But you cannot have a team without a coach, nor a coach without a team. Change the nature of the congregation from an institution to a team, and you change the role of the clergy. Change the role of the clergy to the role of coach, and you change the self-perception of the congregation.

Rebuilding
the Team

The media gathers in the pressroom for an important announcement. The favorite team is in the midst of the longest losing streak in club history. The great players who once carried the team are getting older. The daring tactics that used to win games are no longer effective. The fans are critical, the team is demoralized, and the coach is unhappy. The media agent for the team stands before the microphone: "Today we have begun the process of rebuilding the team. Changes will be made. Some of them will be hard. But in time, we believe this franchise will once again lead the league."

Announcements like that are common in sports. Indeed, great universities, great symphonies, and great corporations have made such announcements. It is time that such announcements become normative for Christian congregations. However one measures success, most Christendom congregations have been on the longest losing streak in denominational history:

- decreasing worship attendance
- smaller Sunday schools
- aging participants
- less outreach
- closure

The laity are demoralized, the clergy are unhappy, and the fans are beyond critical: they have given up.

The biggest mental shift in the postmodern world is that church leaders need to stop longing for institutional renewal and start working to rebuild the team.

The next biggest shift is that church leaders need to recognize that their situation is more like amateur sports than professional sports. Although rebuilding the team might mean replacing the coach, trading older players away, or drafting new talent, the reality in amateur sports is:

- the coach you have is as good as you can get,
- the players you have are the ones who show up,
- the talent you want is already there—just buried.

It might help to hire new clergy, force the resignations of dysfunctional laity, or nominate new members. Yet even professional sports leagues have discovered that, in the end, there is no substitute for the transformation of what you have. So you are the coach. How do you rebuild the team?

Chapter Four

Counterbalanced Leadership

> The first step toward changing your church is to stop loving your church. Love Christ more.

Whenever a coach sets out to rebuild a team, the first thing he or she does is gather a cadre of leaders who all share the same desire. This is why team rebuilding frequently starts with the hiring, firing, redeployment, and retraining of staff or key volunteers. The coach must have a core group who share the same values, who are prepared to take the same risks, and who are ready to run headlong in the same mysterious direction.

Prior to rebuilding, core leadership is often very stable, if not harmonious. They like one another, and even if they do not always agree, they have learned how to get along with each other or get around each other. Once rebuilding begins, this harmony is broken. A new unity, based on very different goals, values, and behavioral expectations, is introduced. The coaching configuration (including the trainers, equipment managers, front office publicists, and all their assistants) must change.

Most modern Christendom churches expect a new or renewing pastor to fit in with the existing staff and core volunteers and, at most, to make evolutionary changes. However, if you really want to transform a church in the postmodern world, you must face the reality that this no longer works. The game of life is moving too fast. Therefore, it is the existing staff and core volunteers who must fit in with the vision of the leader or be replaced. This can be done gently and justly, and it can be done in the context of denominational polity and congregational constitution, but it must be done. And it must be done quickly.

Fortunately, many existing staff and core volunteers are healthy, flexible people who would not still be there if they did not agree with the decision to rebuild the team. They can be mentored, guided, trained, and encouraged. Provided they place themselves on a fast-track, high-learning curve, they can take the time to adapt. Unfortunately, some existing staff and core volunteers are unprepared to change. Perhaps they are unhealthy people with a need to control. Perhaps they are healthy people who just do not like the new direction of the team. Regardless, they must be replaced.

Inevitably, the former staff and core volunteers, and their personal advocates in the congregation, will raise an alarm. In sports, they will say, "This isn't in the great tradition of the New York Yankees that won the World Series several decades ago!" In the church, they will say, "But are we being faithful?"

How to Address the Question of Faithfulness

*But are we being **faithful**?* Living between radical imagination and obsessive timidity as we are, that is a good question. The first thing a good coach must do is *expect* the question. It is astonishing how many leaders are surprised by the question. Their assumptions seem so sound, their interpretations seem so correct, and their goals seem so obvious, that skepticism never occurs to them. Yet skepticism is the new mental "default setting" in the twenty-first century. Whether people are agnostics or true believers, seekers or institutional members, all greet change with cynicism.

Consider a simple decision faced by many small churches today that are maintaining expensive edifices. The roof is leaking so badly that the interior plaster is being damaged and the communion bread is getting moldy! What will we do?

▲ The premodern answer: Let's replace the thatch on our own homes with slate, and build *the grandest roof* Christendom has ever seen—complete with gargoyles.
▲ The modern answer: Let's start a pledge campaign to give a percentage of our discretionary income, and build *the cheapest roof* Christendom has ever seen—complete with eaves troughs.
▲ The postmodern answer: *Why do we need a roof?*

These responses have parallels for every decision, small or large, faced by the congregation, including choices in worship and music, curriculum and program, and personnel. Does faithfulness mean blowing the budget for God, trimming the budget for God, or eliminating the budget for God?

The second thing a good coach must do is *ask* the question. It is amazing how many leaders react to the question but never raise it themselves. They are so certain, so passionate, and so serious that self-doubt seems like a sin. Yet self-criticism is emerging as the most significant, and most difficult, task of spiritual leaders today. In the most dynamic, creative, and growing churches today, the staff and lay leaders spend more time wondering if they are doing the right thing than ever before.

Consider the agenda of the annual congregational meeting. The church is surrounded by challenges and culture is competing for the attention of our youth. What will we do?

▲ The premodern answer: *Let's send to the home office for help and launch a crusade!*

▲ The modern answer: *Let's upgrade our curriculum and hold our staff more accountable.*

▲ The postmodern answer: *Why do we deserve the attention of youth anyway?*

These responses explain why traditional congregational meetings are the last place to begin coaching change. The skepticism that is the default setting of the public disillusions people about the effectiveness of programmatic change, and the unwillingness of church leaders to examine fundamental issues of identity and vision blocks people from systemic change.

The difference between the modern world and the postmodern world lies in *who* is raising the question. In the modern era, the church members raised it, and the church leaders defended themselves. In the postmodern era, the church leaders raise it, and the church members cross-examine themselves.

Are we being faithful? The same question that so often is used as a deterrent to change can be used as an incentive to change. Initially the question is asked out of obsessive timidity. Church leaders fear change and want to draw people back to certainty, comfort, and security. As change accelerates, the same question is asked, but this time it is asked out of radical imagination. Church leaders welcome (or at least accept) change and want to experience it with hope and address it with integrity.

How can we tell when Christian faith is being diluted or enhanced?

When does the quest for relevance become an act of accommodation?

Who can tell when the boundary between imagination and fanaticism is crossed?

Who can tell when the boundary between caution and dysfunction is crossed?

In the millennium world, individual leaders are not
trusted to answer these questions alone—and they do
not trust themselves to answer these questions alone.

Are we being faithful? Regardless of who raises the
question, there is a definite change in expectation about
who is qualified to answer it. Consider the claims to
faithfulness:

▲ The premodern answer: *Whatever our ancestors were,*
we are too.
▲ The modern answer: *Whatever we are, we are not like*
them.
▲ The postmodern answer: *Whatever we are becoming, we*
are not there yet.

Premodern people trusted seminary professors, clergy,
and other certified ecclesiastical leaders to know what
our ancestors believed and did so that we could believe
and do the same things. Modern people trusted competent professionals, denominational offices, and middle
judicatories to know the organizational polity and politically correct liturgy so that we could distinguish
ourselves from everybody else. Postmodern people,
however, do not really know exactly what they will
believe or how they will behave in the mysterious future.

This uncertainty is why postmodern church leaders
living between radical imagination and obsessive timidity do not see themselves as guardians of tradition or
articulators of a denominational ethos. They understand
themselves to be coaches. In the end, integrity is a project for the whole people of God in the context of intense
spiritual growth. Answers to the deepest questions
about faithfulness will be discovered in the midst of

unexpected partnerships and surprising revelations as the followers of Jesus find God's future together.

Counterbalanced Faithfulness

I once saw a photograph from an archaeological dig in Egypt. A huge stone blocked the entrance to a newly discovered tomb of the pharaohs. The chief archaeologist, covered in dust, stood in the trench coaching the efforts of the crew. A lever was placed on a fulcrum. The laborers all gathered to add their counterbalanced strength to the lever. The stone was just beginning to rise. Every eye was straining to penetrate the inner darkness to see what surprising treasures were hidden. The same hope was etched on every eager face in the team. The discoveries in the tomb might rewrite history, alter our understanding of the known world, and redefine our dreams for the future.

Similarly, Christian explorers are sifting through the ruins of a once mighty Christendom. A lever has been placed before the spiritually inert mass of the church. A coach coordinates the efforts of the team. The core leaders gather excitedly to lend their weight to the lever. A gap is beginning to open. What lies inside will make history. And just before the coach shouts, "Push!" someone else with an air of authority shouts, "Stop! Maybe we should just leave things as they are! *Are we really being faithful?*"

In order to use a lever, you need a fulcrum, a sturdy plank or metal bar, and a weight to help you bear down on the bar. This weight is a counterbalance. It magnifies your own strength as you press down the bar and lift the extremely heavy object at the other end. You might be able to lift that heavy object without a counterbalance, but you would need an extraordinarily long metal bar. If the heavy object is a spiritually inert church, the length of that bar would require far more money and time than most church leaders have available. Therefore, you need to add an extra weight to your efforts: a counterbalance to the object at the other end.

The counterbalance is the new perspective that has been embedded in the core leaders of the church. Eventually, everyone in the church will share this counterbalanced faith. Initially, it is the core leaders, the ones who eagerly place their hands on the long metal bar and push hard, who communicate and model that faith. Others may stand and watch as the church is slowly resurrected, and still others may rush to the opposite side of the lever to hold it down. As the core leaders lend their weight to the lever, others catch the fever of anticipation and join.

Yet there is a difficulty! On the whole, modern Christians prefer a balanced faithfulness. Sacred space and secular space, sacred time and secular time dependably support the rhythms of life. Modern Christianity is nothing if not tidy, orderly, and reasonable. When faithfulness is balanced, there are no religious fanatics, nor are there any rabid materialists. Aspects of life can be separated into two powers that balance each other: the church and the state, the clergy and the laity, the Sabbath and the other six days of the week, the taxable and the tax-exempt; even the offering envelope is neatly divided between mission and maintenance. Modern Christians long for a moderately paced, reasonably moral, safe, secure workweek and a nice, intergenerational, predictable, educational experience of the Holy on Sunday morning.

A balanced faith tends to marginalize ancient monks and hermits, iconoclasts and reformers from historical continuity with their congregation. They ignore the utopian revolutionaries and frontier pioneers who may have founded the very congregations that now prize the civilized, homogenized, ritualized balance between the legitimate business of the church and the rest of legitimate society. Whatever founding pioneers might have contributed to mission in the past, they are probably not suitable to be the associate minister or youth director of the Christendom church today.

Modern Christians are prepared to risk their lives for Christ if a Viking berserker or other terrorist breaks into Sunday worship and demands that they recant their faith. However, since modern Christians do not encounter many marauding Vikings in daily life, their balanced faith invites them to enjoy inspiring stories of sacrifice during the sermon and then sends them home for Sunday dinner.

Modern Christians are prepared to risk their livelihoods for Christ if an inspired prophet convinces them that their career must be sacrificed for the common good. However, since few, if any, modern Christians work in jobs that are unambiguously and entirely good or evil, their balanced faith demands only that they try to be nice to their neighbors, fair in the office, and committed to percentage giving in the church pledge campaign.

Yet the postmodern world is more barbaric than civilized. A terrorist just might hold hostages for their faith, and the postmodern image of the global village reveal that our best-considered career paths still harm too many people. Sunday morning promises and percentage giving do not work in an uncivilized world. The happy balance between the sacred and the secular and between the Christian liturgical year and the daily lifestyles of ordinary people has been shattered by a larger discontent.

In the postmodern world, unbalanced church leaders shape an entire lifestyle around Christ. The life and mission of Jesus shape both spontaneous and intentional behavior. Intimate relationships, chance encounters, career paths, vacation plans, personal and family financial planning, diet, housing, transportation, communication, and entertainment are all touched and shaped by a Christian commitment. The test of faithfulness is to prepare oneself for the unpredictable intrusions of radical evil by making every planned and unplanned moment susceptible to the in-breaking of God.

The surrender of an entire lifestyle to God looks suspiciously like fanaticism to a balanced faith. It is excessive. It is what "foreign" religions do. It is perhaps cultic. The greatest criticism the modern church brings to this new behavior of core leaders is not that it is wrong, but that it is unbalanced. This new breed of core leaders actually prefers to be "unbalanced." They choose to shape faith around their lifestyle rather than their institution. Modern church leaders cannot understand this, and this is precisely why even the best-intentioned modern church leaders cannot change the church.

The core leaders you need to rebuild the team do not rely on a balanced faith to change the world. They rely on a counterbalanced faith. One must step outside the hand-in-glove relationship between the church, as a social institution, and the rest of society. A counterbalanced faith increases leverage for change.

Crossing the Boundary to Postmodern Faith

Christendom	Millennium
Systematic Theology	Pragmatic Theology
Propositional Thinking	Metaphorical Thinking
Judicious Evaluation	Experiential Witness
Denominational Heritage	Congregational Identity
Standardized Liturgical Religion	Contextual Spiritual Expression
Professionally Interpreted Scripture	Amateurly Articulated Scripture
Leadership by Office and Competency	Leadership by Credibility and Vision

If you want to leverage change in the church, you must embed a counterbalanced faith in your core church leaders. This is not the traditional faith of memorized catechisms, repetitious worship, and historic creeds. It is not an institutional faith of managed programs and generic mission funds. It is a faith that is integrated with daily lifestyle and that will mark you and your congregational leaders as different, odd, extreme, "off the wall," "out on the edge," and, yes, unbalanced people in the church board room, the office at work, and the shopping mall.

What are the marks of a counterbalanced faith?

Pragmatic Christology

Leaders who leverage change in the church center their lives on a simple, practical companionship with Jesus. It is simple in that it is an easily articulated, perhaps even childlike, devotion to Christ. It is practical in that such companionship pervades every aspect of daily behavior, conversation, and decision making. It is an obsessive preoccupation with the person and with the significance of the historic and timeless figure of Jesus.

- This obsession with Jesus contrasts sharply with the systematic, doctrinal presentations of a balanced faith. Such formulations tend to be intricate—carefully defining ambiguities and clarifying limitations so that the offensiveness of Christ will lose its sting in a society of multifaith and no faith. A counterbalanced faith seeks not to be understandable but to be persuasive.

- The authority of the systematic theology of a balanced faith lies in its institutional character. It is defined by experts and encourages a passivity among the hearers who accept what they can never really comprehend. The authority of counterbalanced Christology is both personal and communal, and it invites vigorous interaction among the companions of Jesus.

Metaphorical Imagining

Leaders who leverage change in the church reflect in metaphor, image, and song. They express meaning by drawing pictures, telling stories, or creating musical harmonies. In so doing, they resemble artists more than philosophers. Key metaphors shape their self-image and define their leadership style. The meaning they point to always escapes mere words, and the import of their metaphors seems to overflow every effort to contain it.

- This fascination with metaphor contrasts sharply with the propositional thinking of a balanced faith. Truth tends to be one-dimensional, communicated in complete sentences (often with several subordinate clauses), and downright wordy. Since it is grammatically correct, it is relatively safe. The Holy can be contained in a box, contained on an altar, or enshrined in a book. A counterbalanced faith uses metaphor to allow the Holy to shatter all efforts to contain it.

- The power of metaphorical imagining lies in its ability for synthesis, not analysis. It combines what appeared to be opposites to reveal an unexpected, underlying unity. Balanced faith does just the reverse, separating seeming similarities to reveal distinct differences. Thus every sermon contains at least three points! Counterbalanced faith relies on a ballad and a bard rather than a sermon and a preacher.

Experiential Witness

Leaders who leverage change in the church talk of what they have heard and seen. They speak in the first person, saying "I" and "we." They approach all conversations as a minority, and therefore expect and invite criticism from those who do not share their assumptions. They tend to be aggressive, not easily dissuaded, and blatantly honest.

- Such witness appears to be arrogance to a balanced faith. Balanced faith talks of what others have heard and seen. They speak in the third person, saying "he," "she," or "they," and this constant reference to other authorities ends by speaking in the second person saying "you." They approach conversations as a majority and only respect criticism from within the circle of orthodoxy. They tend to be smug, occasionally defensive, and benevolently diplomatic. Balanced faith says: *Because they believed this, you should do that.* Counterbalanced faith says: *Because I experienced this, we can do that.*

- The originality of a counterbalanced faith lies in its fresh understanding of power. It differentiates not between the powerful and the powerless but between the controller and the empowered. The experiential witness is living proof of the "power of one."

Congregational Identity

Leaders who leverage change in the church build consensus for values, beliefs, vision, and mission with the congregation serving as the primary mission unit of Christ. The identity of the congregation functions like a genetic code that is embedded in every member, team, and leader. Such identity is deliberately created by the participants, and therefore unique in the spectrum of congregational life. It is the foundation of trust that enables risk.

- Unique, passionate, congregational identity is threatening to a balanced faith. It prefers identity to be established by a denominational heritage, and therefore controlled by a bureaucracy beyond the congregation. This is a hierarchy of accountability designed to limit risk. A counterbalanced faith is always a potential embarrassment to the denomination and a threat to the stability of Christendom.

- Counterbalanced faith is radically hopeful. The denomination perceives the present as a threat to a perpetuated past. The future is always threatened. The congregation that is clear about its identity regards the present as pregnant for the future. The future may be unknown, but it is filled with promise.

Contextual Spiritual Expression

Leaders who leverage change in the church begin with the indigenous culture of their community. The culture, language, life practices, and technologies of their own community become the vehicles to express spiritual experience. Relevance is not a goal that religion seeks to attain but the soil from which authentic spirituality grows.

- Balanced faith values uniformity rather than diversity. Worship becomes standardized by common liturgies and hierarchically shaped lectionaries. The cultural forms and technologies of alien cultures become the vehicles for "proper" religious expression. Such uniformity ensures that indigenous communities will not quarrel and that disagreement can be avoided.

- The dynamism of contextual spiritual expression lies not just in its originality but in its ownership. It emerges from the spiritual formation of the people and is not imposed upon the spiritual formation of the people. It redefines what it means to feel at home in one's faith. Balanced faith replicates standardized practices in every church so that wherever the Christian goes to worship he or she will feel right at home. Counterbalanced faith grows spirituality afresh in each locality so that whenever a Christian returns to God for strength he or she will feel right at home.

Amateurly Articulated Scripture

Leaders who leverage change in the church are not only biblically literate but also biblically conversant. They are disciplined in their reading, but more significant, they are quite spontaneous in applying scripture to everyday experiences. They encounter scripture in their own experiences with the intersection of culture and spirit and, therefore, apply scripture with greater poignancy and daring.

- Balanced faith relies on salaried professionals trained in the seminary to interpret scripture for the people. The people are not expected to work at it, just to listen to it. Professionals interpret scripture from their knowledge of history and their allegiance to denominational tradition. The application of scripture may be sharp, but the cutting edge is wielded by professionals who are not predisposed to hurt anybody. Like dangerous stunts on television, biblical reflection in a balanced faith warns the amateur not to do it.

- The "danger" in amateurly interpreted scripture is that it embeds the stories of Jesus into the contemporary lifestyles of workplace, home, and playground. It leads ordinary people to do radical, unreasonable things without forethought. In a sense, counterbalanced faith risks heresy all the time, because it thrives in the pragmatism of life rather than the purity of thought. Unbalanced, postmodern church leaders prefer a passionately risked mistake to a tepid, intellectual certainty.

Leadership by Credibility and Vision

Leaders who leverage change in the church model the intentionally defined core values, beliefs, vision, and mission of the congregation in their lifestyles. They have adjusted the cadence of their daily walk to the rhythm of the "song in the heart" that is the biblical vision which has seized the congregation. The credibility of lifestyle is more influential than any set of skills because it allows a leader to be more readily adaptable to a rapidly changing culture. Vision is like a compass setting for explorers in the wilderness. No matter what unexpected challenge emerges or what new skill is required, counterbalanced leaders serenely throw themselves into change.

- Balanced faith relies on the credibility of office and the competency of staff. They manage an agenda, repeat and fine-tune programs, and copy behavior patterns. Balanced leaders scramble to follow a timetable, but counterbalanced leaders wait to discern good timing. Balanced faith defends an office and excuses a personality. It is far safer. The greatest risk a leader faces is the need to do counseling or attend continuing education. Counterbalanced faith stakes the parsonage and the pension plan on vision.

- The productivity of visionary leadership is enormous. First, it allows leadership to multiply in entrepreneurial teams rather than waste time in supervised task groups. Second, it places the leader in a constant peril of obsolescence and pushes him or her to constant spiritual growth. In the postmodern world, a clearly focused opportunist influences the world more profoundly than any skilled manager.

The scandal of a counterbalanced faith is that it exaggerates the importance of some aspects of the Christian life and minimizes the importance of others. It is faith "askew." Surely systematic theology, propositional thinking, judicious evaluation, denominational heritage, common liturgy, professionalism, and competency are important, too! A counterbalanced faith recognizes that these are important, but that they have been enslaved by

Christendom and rendered impotent for change. In the end, the greatest criticism of a counterbalanced faith is that it is not balanced. That is the point. It isn't balanced. It is unbalanced. And that is why it leverages change.

Those core leaders who would coach change must not be distracted by those trendy voices that claim to live in a "both-and" world. Such claims arise not from the metaphorical imagining that I have included in a counterbalanced faith, but from a continuing addiction to a balanced faith that simply wants to have its cake and eat it, too. The life and teaching of Jesus reflects his goal to reunite disparate people, synthesize culture and faith, accept people who were formerly unacceptable, and revitalize the spirit of the law. In order to get there, however, Jesus needed to challenge the Pharisees, establish new behavior patterns, separate the sheep from the goats, and replace an old vision with a new one. In order to achieve a truly both-and world, counterbalanced leaders must model and articulate "either-or" choices.

The first step toward changing your church is to stop loving your church. Love Christ more. That is the key message core leaders must understand and proclaim.

Chapter Five

Mature Players

> Adult spiritual growth must become as natural for congregational participants as other forms of healthy exercise.

The reason football coaches appreciate pre-season games is that these events give new players an opportunity to demonstrate their potential and earn a place in the starting line. Whether they are young players newly drafted, veteran players recently traded, injured players newly healed, or old players feeling rejuvenated, the pre-season games give them a chance to show what they can do. In one such game, the Minnesota Vikings were testing a new wide receiver who had been among the top draft choices of the season. His performance was inconsistent. He made brilliant catches and clumsy fumbles. He ran complicated patterns and committed stupid penalties. The most worrisome habit, however, was that whenever he ran back a kick he always stepped out of bounds just before being tackled. He never put his head down to rush for a few more yards and risk getting pounded. The coach's conclusion? "He's young still; he just needs to mature." Unfortunately for the player and for the Minnesota Vikings, the media commentators were still saying the same thing about his plays near the end of the season when his performance continued to be inconsistent!

Once the leaders have learned to counterbalance their faith, the key to change is disciplined adult spiritual formation. We talk about leverage points in the various subsystems of congregational life, but adult spiritual growth is the fulcrum over which everything must be elevated. It is impossible to get very far in expanding worship options, building ministry teams, multiplying cell groups, launching capital campaigns, or renewing property and technology without engaging a majority of the adults in the congregation in serious adult spiritual growth.

This, of course, is also the key problem. The bottom line in many Christendom churches today is that their adult participants really and truly do *not* want to grow spiritually. *I did my catechism as a teenager for confirmation ...I've been to Sunday school...I know I am saved...I know pretty much everything I need to know...I'm about as mature as I need to be ...I don't really need to prioritize my time and shape my lifestyle for personal spiritual growth!* Taken as a group, Christendom people do not really want to grow. They are unwilling to do much more than attend Sunday worship irregularly, participate in the every member pledge campaign, serve a committee, and give money to pay somebody else to do mission.

If this sounds harsh, I suggest that you survey your own congregation in two ways.

- First, do a formal survey asking members over age eighteen to check off the daily and weekly spiritual practices they build into their lifestyles—*excluding* table grace. The list may include daily Bible reading, personal and family prayer, intentional reading and theological reflection, intentional conversation about faith, and so forth. The list may also include weekly participation in a cell group, a hands-on mission or ministry, or a prayer partnership. The results indicate that as few as 2 percent and usually no more than 8 percent, of the adults in a traditional Christendom church are involved in disciplined spiritual growth.

- Second, do an informal survey with a team of volunteers. Simply ask adult members during coffee hour to describe the regular spiritual practices they intentionally build into their daily and weekly routine. Note the time lag as Christendom adults try to figure out what this question even means. A few will brighten immediately and tell you about their Bible reading resource or prayer plan. Most will look blank or say: *"What is a spiritual discipline?" "I didn't know I should be doing anything!" "I never miss my committee meetings!"* or *"What are you, some kind of religious fanatic?"*

Christendom churches all tend to "front load" their adult education by insisting new members take baptism training courses, membership assimilation classes, or catechisms aimed at youth. Thereafter adults are rarely expected to do anything for continuing spiritual growth.

What are the implications? Lack of adult spiritual discipline forces Sunday morning worship to function as the single Christian adult education opportunity in the adult participant's week and leads the church to become obsessive about youth groups. It makes it harder to recruit Sunday school teachers and other volunteers and leads to chronic operating deficits every autumn. It reduces the creative imagination of the church to respond quickly to changing culture and emerging crises and relegates laity to the role of fund-raiser.

Perhaps the most serious implication is that lack of adult spiritual discipline creates a vacuum that declining church leadership fills with obsessive control. As the congregation declines, leaders panic and say, *We just have to do something!* What they choose to do is institutional management; what they should do is disciplined spiritual growth. The former leads to control because the personal tastes, opinions, perspectives, and lifestyles of individual leaders are uncritically imposed on the church in the course of management. The latter leads to freedom because personal preferences are surrendered to a greater experience of the Holy. Many denominations and congregations talk nobly about moving from maintenance to mission, but few are aware that disciplined *adult* spiritual growth is the bridge to get there. Obsession with children's Sunday school and youth groups will not do it.

Opportunity Knocks

The good news is that whenever you identify a fundamental problem, you also uncover a golden opportunity. If a lack of disciplined adult spiritual formation suppresses programs and ministries, renewed focus on spiritual formation can revitalize programs and ministries. This emphasis alone can renew the church, even without additional program initiatives or capital risks.

Church consultants have long pointed out that adult spiritual formation and leadership development go hand in hand. These days one cannot simply recruit volunteers based on their obligation to the institution. They will volunteer only if they are motivated within their own hearts. How can they hear a call if they are not ready to grow? The more intentional they are about growth, the more likely it is they will hear God's call and respond. The self-discipline of growth will make them more readily trainable for excellence and more patient to endure inevitable setbacks in mission.

Evidence suggests that if you just increase commitment to disciplined adult spiritual growth by 10 percent, congregational creativity and spontaneity to mission will increase dramatically. You may not only raise money for distant hurricane victims, but may actually send trained volunteers to help. It will become easier to find Sunday school teachers and youth group leaders. In fact, if teens see their parents taking spiritual growth seriously, you might be able to create a youth group without worrying about which boys and girls are dating each other at any given time. Chronic operating deficits can be eliminated. The Sunday worship service can become the motivational experience God intended rather than the dry, didactic classroom experience it has become.

More important, adult spiritual growth tends to free the church from obsessive control and shifts the leadership focus away from maintenance toward mission. A deeper, shared understanding of values, beliefs, vision, and mission emerges to widen the boundaries of creativity. Adult spiritual growth gives church leaders greater courage to take financial and programmatic risks.

In the declining churches of Christendom, the mission of the church tended to be imposed by congregational or denominational controllers. Imposed mission is almost always timid because preservation of control over the mission agenda is more important than the mission itself. In thriving post-Christendom churches, mission emerges from the spiritual formation of the people. It is almost always more daring because the mission itself is all important. The point of adult spiritual formation is to allow God to "get out of hand" and do unexpected things with the church. Trust is primarily invested not in offices, boards, and management but in the depth and integrity of the spirituality of the leadership.

So stop prioritizing all your energy, budget, and anxiety for children's Sunday school and youth groups and start prioritizing it for adult spiritual formation. In the end, your children and youth will benefit even more.

The Hidden Addiction

If adult spiritual formation is so wonderful, why aren't more Christendom churches emphasizing it? The block to adult spiritual growth is the corporate addiction of the Christendom church to staff dependencies. Laity have been encouraged to see themselves as needy people who require the compassionate care of salaried and certified experts. Clergy have been encouraged to see themselves as religious professionals whose job is to "take care of" the laity. The clergy visit and visit and visit to hold every adult's hand through each life stage until death. The laity waits to be visited—or tells the professional whom to visit—or manages the remaining motivated visitation teams. This terrible codependency blocks adult spiritual formation.

Laity expect the minister to be the spiritually disciplined one. The *laity's* discipline is institutional management. Too often they describe their spiritual journey in the church by listing all the offices and committees they have served. Meanwhile, the Christendom clergy have also assumed they need to be the spiritually disciplined ones. They need a higher continuing education budget than laity, more retreat opportunities than laity, and greater control over worship and liturgy than laity. Too often clergy describe their spiritual journey in the church with complaints that needy laity are holding them back. Behind all of this, laity have become convinced that they can only be the recipients of grace, never the sharers of grace, and clergy have become convinced that they can only be givers of grace, never partners in grace.

The codependency of "needy" laity and clergy who "need to be needed," blocks commitment to adult spiritual formation. Emphasis on adult spiritual formation raises the stress level for everyone. Deep inside, Christendom laity believe that disciplined adult spiritual growth *is not their job*. Deep inside, Christendom clergy are afraid that spiritually growing adults *will usurp their role.*

•◦ Laity think: *If I grow spiritually, I many have to think for myself, take initiative in ministry, and live like I really am in a mission field.*
•◦ Clergy think: *If those adults grow spiritually, someone will preach better sermons than I do, be welcomed in hospital visitation more warmly than I am, gain more authority in Bible study classes than I have, and pray more effectively in public than I can.*

Therefore, Christendom laity vastly prefer to receive Holy Communion than to share it with others. They prefer sermons be preached at them rather than share faith with others. They would rather pay experts to do ministry rather than discern and do the quality mission that they are gifted and called to do. The tragedy is that *Christendom clergy prefer that, too!* If lay adults grow spiritually, clergy entitlements will be lost, clergy egos will be bruised, and clergy may need to retrain to become instructors of mission instead of doers of ministry.

The last thing codependent Christendom churches really want is disciplined adult spiritual formation. They believe it is far better to be preoccupied with children's Sunday schools, insist on teen confirmation, hire a youth minister, and enjoy the myth that the youth are the future of our church.

Freeing Adults to Grow

Once the problem has been defined, the opportunity becomes clear. Adult spiritual formation will not only revitalize programs and ministries, but it will ultimately shatter the unhealthy codependency that has disempowered church leadership during the twentieth century. What will it take to seize this opportunity? We can take our clues from other addiction relief programs.

❑ **It will take courage.** Enter adult spiritual formation knowing that it will be stressful. The real stress is not that it will change your timetable but that it will change your life, your leadership roles, and your church.

❑ **It will take partnerships.** Do spiritual disciplines in pairs, triads, or cell groups. As in every other form of exercise, success is more likely in the context of mutual understanding and support. Do not try to read your Bible, pray, or meditate alone. Do it with a team.

❑ **It will take repetition.** Promote, recognize, and celebrate spiritual disciplines constantly—not just on a few Sunday mornings. Create an environment for spiritual growth, just as you have developed an environment of committee life and denominational ethos.

❑ **It will take modeling leadership.** Key board members and core lay leaders need to step up, go public, and articulate their own spiritual disciplines before the congregation. Tell stories, share successes and failures, joys and frustrations. Train your core lay leaders to be coaches for spiritual growth.

❑ **It will take God's power.** As with all addictions, only the intervention of a higher power will finally liberate the Christendom church from the addiction of staff dependency. Pray for it in board and staff meetings. Talk about it with expectation. It may happen when you are most doubtful that it will ever come.

The goal is that adult spiritual growth will become as natural for congregational participants as other forms of healthy exercise. It should go beyond time management and become spontaneous behavior. It is simply the way one lives, the way one commutes to work, the way one interacts with family, and the way one organizes his or her weekly timetable.

Adult Spiritual Discipline in a Postmodern World

When I was a lad my spiritual discipline was built around a print curriculum and the segregation of my sacred time from the rest of daily life. I used *The Upper Room* devotional guide, a Genesis-to-Revelation Bible reading program, occasional Sunday worship, and summer camp. It was a classic discipline for the mind—accomplished in quiet retreat from the rush of daily life.

The twenty-first century, however, is a different world, and as my son and daughter grow to adulthood, their spiritual disciplines will look different. Their spiritual practices are built around interactive video, audio, and CD-ROM. The boundaries between sacred and secular time have vanished into a single continuum. It is a discipline for the mind, heart, and body—accomplished in the rhythm and rush of daily living.

What will postmodern spiritual discipline look like? It will still be centered on the Bible, and it will bring people into a closer relationship with Christ. From there, the options will be as many as there are Christians. Here are some clues:

- *Lifestyle based:* Spiritual disciplines will be oriented not around a curriculum but around life experiences. They will not only adjust lifestyle but will be shaped by lifestyle. Demographic realities of race, gender, marital status, and age—and psychographic realities of taste, attitude, and music—will customize individual disciplines.

- *Holistic:* Spiritual disciplines will not simply train the mind. They will integrate relationship with God, self, and intimate others. Spirituality and healthy living will be interrelated. Physical, mental, emotional,

Postmodern Spiritual Discipline
Lifestyle Based
Holistic
Customized by Culture
Metaphoric
Tecnhology Supported
Partnered and Networked
Action-reflection

relational, and spiritual well-being will be the goal of every individual's discipline.

- *Customized by culture:* Spiritual disciplines will not seek to fortify the will to resist the temptations of culture. They will shape an intuition that perceives God in, and through, culture. Ethnic orientation and cross-cultural ideas, practices, and behavior will make spiritual formation more contextual or indigenous than ever before. Culture itself will become a vehicle, not a barrier, to the infinite.

- *Talisman, symbol, metaphor, and mantra:* Spiritual disciplines will not practice a principle but live out a metaphor. They will not defend a theological perspective but elaborate variations on a theme. In the postmodern world, adult spiritual formation resembles jazz improvisation, not Gregorian chant. Images and objects will replace abstractions and dogmatic propositions as the focus of meditation.

- *Technology supported:* Spiritual disciplines will not be accomplished through print media and spoken words alone. The computer will integrate images and sounds, sur-rounded in multiple forms of music, in all instrumen-tations imaginable. Do you remember how that worn leather Bible, inherited from your parents, became a companion and comfort in your spiritual growth? The computer system and portable CD player will be as central to the spiritual disciplines of the next genera-tions.

- *Partnered and networked:* Spiritual disciplines will not be "atomic" but "molecular." Individuals will not do it alone but in partnerships of intimacy and hon-esty that intentionally cross old demographic bound-aries. Clergy will not pursue spiritual disciplines with other clergy but with CEOs from nonprofit and cor-porate organizations. Adults will not only join with members of their church but with associates in the workplace and people of other faiths. More than this, they will partner with others around the world through the emerging intimacy of the Internet.

- *Action-reflection model:* Spiritual disciplines will not be retreats but activities. Meditation and risk will be united. Insights will be tested in the mission field, re-examined, and tested again. Work will become its own crucible of spiritual growth and the commute back home its own opportunity for reflection—supported by surround-sound audio systems and air-condition-ing.

In the end, Christian formation in the postmodern world will not really be a *spiritual discipline* at all; it will be a *spiritual life*. The boundaries between sacred time and secular time, sacred space and secular space, will disap-pear. People will not practice spiritual growth at specific times or in particular settings, but they will embed it into daily routine and seemingly mundane places.

If you want to coach change in the postmodern world, do not start by taking the entire board away on a retreat into the woods. Do not insist that all individuals or groups study a common curriculum. Do not assume that spiritual growth is a form of Christian education. Your approach to a congregation with limited commitment to adult spiritual discipline will probably look like this:

◆ Start by doing it yourself. Make it a priority in your own life and demonstrate the value of shaping a lifestyle around God. Talk honestly with others (individually, collectively, in worship) about your own struggles with time and energy, but also talk openly about the fulfillment, joy, and health that it gives you. Even with this, be patient because it is only when your unthinking words and spontaneous actions reveal the positive impact of your spiritual commitment that anyone will take heed.

◆ Look for partners in this quest from the edges or margins of congregational life. Board members are wonderful people, but their very business in managing the institution undermines their credibility as spiritual leaders. The people really committed to a spiritual life tend to resist nominations to the board and move quietly at the fringes of organized religion. Provide opportunities for them to tell their stories.

◆ Present the congregation with as many options as possible, supported by as many technologies as possible, and in as many medias as possible. A Spiritual Resource Fair, for example, can bring together literally hundreds of possibilities from simple to complex, from inexpensive to expensive. Suspend all judgment. The spiritual discipline that works for you may not work for another, and no discipline is better, deeper, or more profound than another. A good spiritual discipline is simply one that works. It does not matter *what* discipline people choose but that they choose something.

◆ Make sure that spiritual disciplines are always partnered. In an era of frustrated dieters and lonely joggers, everyone knows that any discipline is apt to be more successful if it is done with two or three others. Encourage covenants to meet, talk, trade E-mail, or generally encourage, mutually support, and pray for one another as each person does whatever works for them.

◆ Give permission for constant customization and adaptation. Culture is not your enemy but your friend. Use whatever cultural form or life experience best helps to focus attention on one's relationship with God. If you need silence to concentrate, turn the TV off. If you need noise to concentrate, turn up the TV and the radio. If you do your best thinking while driving, drive. Post-Christendom spiritual growth does not require a resource or blueprint to be followed doggedly to the bitter end. It requires constant coaching to adapt to the chaos of daily living. That is why you do it in partnerships.

◆ Encourage adults to anchor their spiritual discipline around an image or metaphor rather than a methodology or resource. Methods and resources are helpful, but you will always be changing and adapting them. A key image or metaphor for spiritual life, however, can both anchor the chaotic experience of constant adaptation and also inspire creativity. Boomers may choose a mantra, and echoes may choose a talisman, but the centrality of a particular metaphor, which constantly lurks at the edges of the mind, provides continuity in chaos. Post-Christendom spirituality is a matter of poetry, not prose.

Adults need to make their life spiritually interactive. Spiritual growth is neither private philosophy nor public piety, but an experience of risk. Questions need to be vocalized, insights need to be tested, and these experiments in applied spiritual living need to be pondered and evaluated. Does this insight make sense in the light of daily life experience? Can daily life experience be made better because of this insight?

Postmodern adults value spiritual formation but with different criteria than adults in the Christendom world. This is because they are asking different questions. Christendom adults of the past measured success by asking:

❑ *Is my life more stable?* They believe spiritual growth should make life predictable, continuous with heritage, and comfortable for daily routine.

❑ *Is my faith more correct?* They believed spiritual growth should make faith denominationally consistent, politically and dogmatically proper, and consistent with hierarchical authorities.

❑ *Is my attitude more obedient?* They believed spiritual growth should make the burdens of institutional maintenance both tolerable and meaningful—so that they could tithe without it hurting too much.

In the postmodern era, however, adults know their lives will never be stable. They do not care if their faith is synchronized with denominational authorities. They feel no sense of duty to maintain an institution. They are only motivated to engage spiritual disciplines if it answers other questions.

The questions postmodern adults ask motivate a different kind of spirituality. They do not expect to know more about God but to experience God. They do not want to live more traditionally but more authentically. They do not want to resist insidious attacks from popular culture but discover the holy in, through, and in spite of popular culture. The post-Christendom measure of success is simple:

Measuring Success

Is my life healthier?

Is my faith more portable?

Is my attitude more optimistic?

- *Is my life healthier?* They believe spiritual growth should positively affect their physical, emotional, mental, and relational health. They think and feel holistically.

- *Is my faith more portable?* They believe spirituality should permeate daily work and leisure, give meaning to routine, and give strength in crisis. They need to take it with them wherever the chaos of life takes them. They want to be confident.

- *Is my attitude more optimistic?* They believe spiritual growth should give one a brighter outlook, a more positive attitude, and a good reason not to commit suicide the next evening. It should help them perceive the in-breaking of God's grace in the environment disaster-zone of Earth. They yearn for hope.

If spiritual disciplines accomplish these goals, postmodern people will embrace them. The choice of the curriculum and the correctness of the method are both secondary. The only real measure of success is that these spiritual disciplines work. They bring joy and fulfillment. They benefit other people and the planet as a whole. Only then will adults prize church involvement.

Chapter Six

Contemporary Equipment

> Technology is more than methodology: it is the way people discover and interpret meaning in life.

The incentive for technological change and the impact of technological change are more clearly seen in sports than in any other social activity. Artificial turf and domed stadiums have transformed the strategies of North American football. New designs in footwear and nonbreakable hoops and backboards have allowed bigger, more acrobatic basketball players to be more aggressive than ever. Tennis rackets made of graphite, field hockey sticks made of laminated plastic and wood, synthetic soccer balls made of more durable and weather resistant material—all these have changed the way games are played. Behind the scenes, advanced computerized training equipment and scientifically designed diets are making players stronger and more resistant to injury.

Golf is perhaps the one sport that talks the most about tradition, yet it makes the most of technological change. In 1899, Findlay S. Douglas (Amateur Champion of the USA) wrote:

> Time deals hard with the golf player of to-day. Fifty years ago a golfer's set contained, at the very most, two iron

clubs, a driving iron and a niblick. Where to-day we use a
cleek, they of the past obtained like results by means of a
spoon, long, middle or short, as the distance required....
      To-day, the average golfer carries six irons in his
bag....
      [And] to be able to play well with the iron clubs is a
most important factor in the game.[1]

For Douglas in 1899, the old debate between apple or
persimmon wood to make short- and middle-range
clubs had given way to a debate between iron or aluminum. The wooden putter had been replaced by one
made of metal. The leather ball had been replaced by the
gutta-percha ball.

Could Douglas have imagined the changes in golf
technology by the end of the twentieth century?
Probably. At least he would have been unafraid of them
because technological innovation was part of the game.
Balanced, cast, and forged clubheads; graphite shafts;
synthetic grips; two-handed putters; treated leather
gloves; long distance balls; scientifically designed golf
courses; test robots and research equipment; video training tapes; and a thousand other innovations have transformed the game. Many people are nostalgic collectors
of golf memorabilia, but how many would enter a tournament still carrying two iron clubs, a niblick, and a
leather ball?

Nonetheless, that is how many modern churches
choose to operate in a technologically advanced, postmodern world. They say they want to change or grow
(attract the youth, increase worship attendance, reach
out to boomers or busters), but they come to their first
golf lesson carrying an antique iron with a hickory shaft
and using code words that nobody understands, like
niblick or narthex. What on earth is the coach to say?
Will he or she say: "Great! Let's spend all our resources
to grow a church for people who love to wear plus fours,
play with niblicks and spoons, and compare everything

to 'The Olde Course' at St. Andrew's?" or will the coach say: "Go buy the right equipment, and when you're really serious about the game let me know!"

Technology and Identity

There is a good reason why historians identify epochs by technology. The Stone Age, the Bronze Age, the Iron Age, the Industrial Age, the Atomic Age, and the Computer Age all label major eras in civilization. It is not only that the people of these times *used* a specific kind of tool, but that their very lives were *redefined* by a specific kind of tool. Technology is more than methodology: it is philosophy. Each new technology is a way to discover and interpret life in a new way.

Consider how technologies have influenced religion. Religion has always used technology to celebrate faith, decorate sanctuaries, and worship divinity. More important, however, is that technology has always shaped religion itself by providing new ways to test ideas and explore life.

▲ In the Stone Age, humans used crude instruments of rock and wood to hunt game, till soil, fight enemies, and decorate caves. If they wandered more than a mile from home, it was at considerable risk. There was no better focus for ancient folk religion than the snake that guarded house and home.[2]

▲ In the Bronze Age, humans fashioned new cooking ware, created beautiful jewelry, built wagons and chariots, and journeyed to Troy and beyond. They had a better diet, more time to philosophize, and the means to trade with the world and interact with other cultures. In the Bronze Age, magnificent temples were constructed and an exodus from Egypt became a definitive moment in religious experience.

▲ In the Iron Age, humans created enduring civiliza-
tions, traveled across oceans, and developed surgical
techniques to help them understand the human body.
They governed both more benevolently and more
cruelly, and they had more leisure to write great liter-
ature and lousy pornography. In such an age, geno-
cide was a reality and an exile to Babylon equaled the
Exodus as the most definitive moment in the religion
of a people.

As epoch followed epoch, both culture and religion
would be transformed by technology. Civilization
moved from papyrus to paper to printing press, and religion moved from proclaimed gospel, to written epistle,
to mass-produced Bible. Refinements in metallurgy,
glass, and the flying buttress blossomed into stained
glass and cathedral architecture. Advances in cheap
manufacturing and construction allowed every denomination to have a church building in every community,
and every building to have an organ.

▲ In the Industrial Age, humans increased productivity,
developed economic systems, lengthened life spans,
and redefined family life. They mass produced both
the necessities and luxuries of daily living and multiple musical tastes could be effectively satisfied for the
first time. Religious denominations multiplied expo-
nentially, a major religious movement so embedded
methodology into its identity as to be labeled
"Methodist," and the quest for civil rights transformed the character of preaching and mission budgets of churches.

▲ In the Atomic Age, humans made big bombs, illuminated enormous cities, cured diseases that had threatened life for centuries, and claimed the moon. They
rendered famine a moral evil, when, previously, it

was just the result of climatic change. The threat of global disaster and the limitless potential for human expansion caused religions to appreciate each other as equals. The boundaries between science, science fiction, religion, spirituality, and chicanery were forever blurred.

▲ In the Computer Age, humans interact with other cultures, download information in seconds, compute solutions to incredibly complex problems, and produce images in a variety of ways that are limited only by the expanding imagination of a seven-year-old. Learning requires all five senses, growth requires the intimacy of a team, and knowledge demands a unity of being. Religious faith is not just a leap but also a leap across a culturally created chasm of selfishness that can only be accomplished in surround-sound when informed by the Internet while holding hands with a true friend.

The point is technology makes possible new ways to discover and interpret life. This, in turn, redefines religious understanding. We do not just worship differently, we think differently. We approach God differently. We interpret life with new metaphors, new needs, new hopes, and new expectations.

Technology not only influences how we think about religion and life, it also sets the speed at which we must think and act. Technology is always pushy, never passive. Humans did not begin working with iron because they *wanted* to. They did it because they *had* to. Most people learn to use the computer grudgingly, not joyfully, because they have no real choice. Technology does not just bring change; it insists on change. The urgency keeps getting faster and faster.

▲ It took five centuries before the novelty of *tempered* steel ceased to be important;
▲ It took one century before the novelty of *homogenized* milk ceased to be important;
▲ It took only one decade before the novelty of *formatted* floppy disks ceased to be important.

No doubt there are still uses for nontempered steel, nonhomogenized milk, and unformatted floppy disks, but can anyone readily think of them? Our language is littered with irrelevant qualifications about technology that are now obsolete. Life is changing faster than we can describe it. If technology is so decisive to how we discover and interpret the world and if technology creates its own urgency to reshape and adapt the way we think and behave, then why does the modern Christendom church ignore technology?

My grandfather was incredibly sensitive to technology and change. He taught English as a second language in 1920s Ohio. He established one of the first radio stations in Cleveland (The call letters WHK are the initials of William Kenneth Carpenter). He owned one of the first pocket radios and one of the first televisions; and my favorite photograph shows him sitting on an early motorcycle with my grandmother in the sidecar. He became a leading layperson in the large Methodist church in the elite Shaker Heights in Cleveland and taught a large adult Sunday school class for years. I have his notes; they are littered with references to new technologies and insights into changing culture. He died prematurely in the 1950s.

Despite such leadership, the churches in Shaker Heights at the turn of the millennium are aging, declining congregations living in beautiful buildings surrounded by stained glass. The pipe organ would have jarred St. Benedict as a cultural aberration, and the central air-conditioning would have troubled John Donne as an accommodation to creaturely comforts, but otherwise they would feel right at home. Where are the video screens? Where are the computer terminals? Where is the surround sound? Where are the cappuccino makers for the post-service coffee hour? Where are the microphones, amplifiers, and film projectors? Where are the technologies that my grandfather foresaw as vehicles to interpret life and proclaim the gospel to a new age?

A United church in St. John's pioneered radio among the outports of Newfoundland. Long before there were highways, when the only link between communities was the sea, this church not only established an early radio transmitter in the steeple. They also helped little outport churches obtain radio receivers. Bitterly resisted in some places as a work of the devil, these receivers eventually established a Christian education link that was one of the first of its kind in North America. When the Canadian Confederation regulated all of the radio stations, the charter specifically protected the church ownership of this station.

Despite that paradigm-shifting leadership, at the turn of the millennium this church is also an aging, declining congregation. They, too, have a beautiful building with curved, hardwood pews and a lovely pipe organ. They recently spent over $80,000 to improve the radio transmitter—but they broadcast classical and traditional religious music. Why not be paradigm-shifting leaders again with the same strategy but different technology? Why not establish a computer center, help all the outports buy computers, and electronically share Christian educational resources and endless varieties of contemporary Christian music?

It is not just that modern Christendom churches do not use new technologies. They actively resist it. They actively resist it despite the pioneering efforts of their own historic leaders. Surrounded by technologies from the fourteenth century through the nineteenth century (all beautifully maintained at significant cost), they wonder why people under thirty-five do not come. Indeed, they fail to see the connection between the increased numbers of seniors on the Internet and the increased number of church veterans dropping out of worship and moving to the margins of congregational life.

Why resist? The common answer is that new technology is, after all, just another methodology—only more expensive. "We can't afford it!" Affordability alone, however, does not explain the bizarre, dogged resistance of the modern church to new technology. The same congregation that believes new technology to be unaffordable spends thousands of dollars from the memorial fund to maintain stained glass and other cutting edge technologies of the twelfth century. The same lay leaders who cannot afford new technology in the church heavily invest in new technology in their homes, businesses, and school systems.

Why resist? The second most common answer still treats new technology as superfluous gadgetry. "We may be able to afford it, but we won't prioritize it! The technology we have is good enough." If only contemporary culture would slow down and learn to appreciate antiques, they would hear the gospel proclaimed. The problem is with cultural attitudes, they believe, not church technologies, and somewhere the church must draw a line about cultural accommodation that it will not cross. Priority alone, however, still does not explain the bizarre, dogged resistance of the modern church to new technology. The same congregations that claim to be satisfied with technologies that are good enough, busily acquire elevators to replace stairs, microwaves to replace stoves, and aluminum roofs to replace shingles. Modern churches cross the line of cultural accommodation all the time, but not to prioritize technology.

Affordability is not the issue, and the attempt to shift responsibility to the waywardness of culture is not credible. What is the real reason for such bizarre, dogged resistance? Deep in their hearts, modern church members do know that technology is more than a methodology. It is indeed a philosophy, and they are terrified.

▲ The old technologies of stained glass, pipe organs, mono-sound, pulpit microphones, pulpits and lecterns, hymnbooks, choir lofts, fixed pews, and all the rest have become addictions. The church is as addicted to them, and to their perpetuation, as a four-pack-a-day smoker is addicted to cigarettes. They cannot let go. They can afford the diet plans, but they will not let go. They prefer inventing a theological boundary between a designated religious smoking area and the rest of the cultural restaurant, and they will not let go. They will deny the truth, avoid the truth, and become angry at the truth, but they will not let go of their addiction.

▲ The old technologies comfortably limit spiritual growth. It is no accident that the same churches that avoid new technologies have far less than 10 percent of their adult participants seriously engaged in disciplined faith formation seven days a week. The addiction to old technology is a powerful tactic to control, regulate, or block the birth of a new idea, the discovery of a fresh insight, or the emergence of a motivating vision. The best way to avoid getting to the moon is to insist that scientists use an abacus. The best way to avoid reaching the Promised Land is to insist that the children of Israel hunker down in the desert and build a pyramid.

The dogged persistence of old technology in the church is a clear sign of an unhealthy spiritual life. Affordability has nothing to do with it. Those old technologies are a blatant public admission: "We don't want to grow. We don't want fresh ideas and new perspectives. We will block you, criticize you, or dismiss you as a sinner caving in to culture if you dare try." The public gets the message. They do not come, they do not join, they do not participate, and, if they are already in the church, they will not stay. *The truth: technology is not about gadgets—it's about growth.*

Technology is not a secondary issue. It is a primary issue. Technology is not just about methodology. It is about the way people discover God and interpret their experiences of the Holy. Technology is not a budget issue—something you spend money on when every other cost has been covered. It is a missions issue—something you spend money on even when you do not have it, because you must.

Technology-Supported Faithfulness

In order to lever a heavy object, one needs a fulcrum and a wooden plank or metal bar. The nature of this latter instrument will limit or magnify your ability to leverage change. If the immovable object is a church, old technologies won't do it. They will either bend or break, and the church won't change. You need an instrument made with a different material, the most contemporary alloy, to lever the church into a new position.

Coaches seeking to change the church cannot be shy or timid about the subject of technology. Do not allow the board discussion to be deflected by arguments about affordability. Focus the debate on the cost of discipleship. Do not allow the clergy to defer decisions about technology in favor of Lenten seminars exploring the abstractions of Christ and culture. That worthy debate has been going on from biblical times and will not be resolved until the Second Coming and to make decisions about new technology contingent on the outcome is simply a dodge to preserve a harmonious pastoral relationship. Focus the debate on the issue of risk.

In order to shift the attitudes of traditional church leaders, concentrate on communicating these two key epochal changes in perspective.

❑ *Twenty-first-century people value technology in the way that twentieth-century people valued property.*

In the previous century, property revealed identity and guaranteed security. That's why property ownership was so important to our parents and grandparents. Exterior architecture and interior decoration revealed the core values of the people who lived there. Their choice of seating, furnishing, color, and light revealed how they thought, believed, and hoped. Property ownership enabled them to control their environment, imprint their identity on public perception, and guarantee that it would endure.

Twentieth-century people take pride in the fact that their church property (exterior and interior) is *incompatible* with the surrounding properties of the community. The gothic buildings jar perception amid the efficient office buildings and illuminated businesses of the downtown area. The rural, one-room buildings with steeples (surrounded by the cemetery) seem out of place among the new municipal halls, renovated public schools, and farms with high-tech machinery parked in the barn. Twentieth-century people like it that way. If the worship center is now more uncomfortable than the average urban apartment or rural cottage and the church basement is draftier than the urban subway or the rural barn, so much the better. The church is supposed to shun the world.

In the twenty-first century, fewer people will own property, and more people will reveal identity and guarantee security through technology. That's why upgrading the media system is so important to our children and grandchildren. Exterior architecture and interior decoration still reveal core values and profound beliefs, but now these must be interactive, adaptable to change, and speak to the heart as well as the mind. Their ability to create virtual surroundings allows them to reveal how they think, believe, and hope. In an impermanent world, technology enables them to shape their environment, imprint their identity on public perception and guarantee that it will be relevant as the community changes.

Twenty-first-century people take pride in the fact that their church technology is *compatible* with the technologies currently used in the community. It allows them to interface with the social services of the city or region. It allows them to transition smoothly from the public school, regional hospital, local or corporate business, or modern kitchen and seamlessly blend spirituality with daily living. The worship center should be equipped with the same quality technology as the family car and farm tractor, or the home recreation room and business office. If the worship center is now as comfortable as an auditorium and living room, and the nursery is as high quality as the community day care center, so much the better. The church is supposed to bridge religion and culture with the gospel.

❑ *Twenty-first-century people value communication in the way that twentieth-century people valued location.*

In the previous century, location revealed integrity and mission. The fact that your parents' or grandparents' church was located on this street, that corner, this neighborhood, or that side of town declared their awareness of the mission field and their urgency to address it. The parish boundary was defined by the railroad, and which side of the tracks you were on defined the mission field.

To be located somewhere was bold, public declaration: *We are here, we are committed, and we will last forever.*

Twentieth-century people built for eternity. The building was a container of eternal truth. They saw themselves as immovable objects in a changing world. Behind all the programs, Sunday schools, and worship services, the primary mission of the church was a ministry of presence. Despite dilapidated structures, demographic shifts, municipal re-zoning, and limited parking, they would not relocate. Even if a fire burned down the building, they would rather rebuild on the same site than move. Relocation would be an admission of defeat.

In the twenty-first century, the airport is the center of mobility, and, at any moment, a new highway might cut across the front yard of your church. The integrity and mission of our children and grandchildren are revealed by their ability to communicate in the languages, symbols, and advertising of the community. It is the ability to speak in words used by other ethnic groups. It is the ability to share ideas and feelings through images, music, computers, and DOS. It is the ability to talk to intimates in the idiom of this week and to strangers in the symbols of global understanding. To communicate well is a bold, public declaration: *We are everywhere, we care, and we will do whatever it takes to reach out.*

Twenty-first-century people build for marketability. The building is a vehicle of effective communication. They see themselves as moving partners in a journey of faith. Behind all the programs and ministries is a determination to tag along—wherever people are going—doggedly pursuing a dialogue about faith. Whether by personal conversation, advertising, radio, television, Internet or E-mail, these people never stop talking. If the location of the building inhibits that conversation, they will sell it and relocate. The power to rapidly upgrade, download, and reboot—or renovate, rebuild, and relocate—enables them to be in continuous mission.

The experience in every epoch of humankind is that the power of religion in life depends on the continuity between the technologies of the religious organization and the way people conduct business and enjoy leisure time.

For modern Christians, "technology-supported faithfulness" is a contradiction in terms. This is not merely motivated by nostalgia and resistance to changing old habits. It is the recognition that technology is not theologically neutral. New technology changes the nature and strategy of church life—just as it has changed the nature and strategy of sports. With new technology, it really is not the same game anymore. Congregational life will not be *quite* the same anymore.

For postmodern Christians, technology-supported faithfulness is the crucial link for the fulfillment of God's destiny for the world. Technological innovation and daring outreach logically point to one another in faithful, postmodern Christian witness. If congregational mission is to succeed, then congregational life must always change. God's call to faithfulness is a call to not preserve a way of life but to accomplish a holy mission.

Abstractly and academically, the modern church has emphasized ecclesiology at the expense of missiology. The postmodern church now emphasizes missiology over ecclesiology. Modern churches look to the past and remember traditional liturgies, gothic architectures, medieval images, local traditions, extended family habits, or nineteenth-century music. They seek to preserve an orthodoxy and ethos that existed more in theory than in fact. Postmodern churches look to the past to learn from the radical innovations, cultural revolutions, and religious reformations that changed the church forever. They seek to advance the mission of God to a higher level of individual awareness and social impact.

The traditional church has always bitterly resisted technology-supported faithfulness. It resisted hermits living in caves, spiritual disciplines using icons, seating for commoners in the nave, Bibles printed in ordinary languages, organs in the sanctuary, hymns with lyrics written for popular tunes, clocks in the belfry, clergy in plain dress, indoor plumbing, automobile parking by the hitching post, electricity in the Sunday school, amplifiers in the pulpit, air-conditioning in the South and oil furnaces in the North, radio broadcasts, televised worship, dishwashers in the kitchen, and elevators to the second floor. Did these technological innovations change the church? Of course they did. Will surround-sound, computer-generated images, and Internet education change the church? Of course they will.

Technology is not theologically neutral, but whether it is beneficial or not depends largely on one's approach to theology. If ecclesiology is the cornerstone of theology, Christians will fear technological change. If missiology is the cornerstone of theology, Christians will welcome technological innovation. Indeed, they will insist upon it. Unless they use the best tools to communicate the gospel and are willing to adjust their budgets, learning patterns, and corporate habits to use those tools with maximum effectiveness, they are no longer being faithful. Ask the daring reformers, some known and many unknown, who initiated the list of changes mentioned above in churches across North America and around the world. They agree.

Apply Technology to Worship

Technology is the instrument of change. That instrument must be applied directly to worship. New technologies applied to church administration, the pastor's sermon preparation, Christian education, or youth programming will not change the church until they have been applied to worship. There is a reason why, in a time of epochal change, the bitterest fights are fought over worship, and it is that worship is the balance of power in congregational life. Change worship, and administration, staff, education, and programming will all have to change as well. Unless worship changes, the technological advances in other aspects of congregational life will be limited or irrelevant.

Those who really want to coach change cannot be timid. The old technologies of worship must be replaced with new technologies. Remember, the reason is not just methodological but philosophical. New technologies in worship will encourage spiritual growth, enliven the church with fresh imagination and vision, and generally reshape the way we think about God and interpret the world.

In order to change the church, worship must become interactive, motivational, and passionate. In order to accomplish this, image, sound, and ambience must be of the same nature and quality that blends with the life experience of people during the week. This requires a choreography of worship, not just a liturgy. It requires an experience that carries participants away, not a printed bulletin that ties participants down. What are some of these changes?

The Choreography of Worship
Image
Sound
Ambience

• *Image.* Video, film, computer-generated images, overhead projections, painting, sculpture, and photographs. You will need computers, software, permanent video screens, LCD projectors, monitors for each worship leader, and a plan to blend images with everything that is being done in worship

- *Sound.* Endless varieties of music, audiotapes, CDs, dialogue, sound effects including everything from whistles to whale song, and clear speaking voices. You will need quantities of wireless microphones, amplifiers, mixers, electronic instruments and room for musicians, surround-sound speakers, DVD capability, and a plan to blend sound with everything that is being done in worship.

- *Ambience.* Variable and colored lighting, fresh air, aromas, thematic decorations, hands-free participation, touchable symbols of faith, freedom of movement, choices about anonymity, and quality food options. You will need remote-controlled lighting, flexible seating, projected announcements, specialty coffees, teas, and juices (and a place to put them during worship), incense or breadmakers, space to dance, multiple options to give to mission, and a plan to create a unique experience in every worship service.

That is a pretty long and dramatic list, and coaches for change will instinctively know they cannot do it all tomorrow. What is even scarier is that this list will be out of date shortly as technologies are upgraded or introduced into the daily living of the public.

Where do you start? Since every context is different, the rule of thumb is that you start wherever the opportunity is greatest and the stress is least. Sometimes you will have to create the opportunity because it will not be handed to you. It may be the place where stress is the *lowest*, but it will certainly not be a place where stress is *absent*. Most coaches already know they need to build support among key staff and lay leaders who understand the issues I have defined in this chapter. Once you have a credible support team ready to jump off the cliff with you, here's what you do:

1. *Start somewhere—now!*

The discontinuity between the technologies of culture and the technologies of the church is vast already. You cannot afford to dither in ad hoc committees. Launch yourselves at the best opportunity, trusting that you will inevitably make adjustments once you are involved. You do not need a strategic plan, and if you had one, it would not work.

2. *Establish boundaries!*

Decentralize the management of change by

How?

1) Start somewhere—now!

2) Establish boundaries!

3) Take small steps, but keep going!

4) Demonstrate first; explain later!

5) Feedback and fine tune!

6) Do everything in spiritual growth teams!

7) Add on, let go, and never go backward!

---

establishing some broad boundaries for action and freeing teams to discern, design, implement, and evaluate what they think must be done. Worship committees that insist on hearing reports, evaluating recommendations, and approving tactics will frustrate leaders and undermine change. Turn people loose.

3. *Take small steps, but keep going!*

You will not accomplish it all overnight, so do not try. Build change incrementally on the change you have already achieved. The key is not to take big steps but to continue taking the little ones. One opportunity will lead to another, but you must resist resting on your laurels and find courage to seize the next challenge. The most important quality of leadership here is not imagination—it is persistence.

4. *Demonstrate first; explain later!*

Experiential worship cannot be explained in words. That is why they call it "experiential"! Don't try to prepare people to understand something ahead of time. Just warn them that it is an experiment, then do it. Demonstrating what you are trying to do, even imperfectly, must precede attempts to explain it.

5. *Feedback and fine tune!*

Once you are doing it, intentionally create opportunities to listen to feedback and keep tinkering with what you are doing until you get it right. Create focus groups of church insiders and outsiders, debrief your various teams immediately after every experiment, talk personally with people who like and do not like what you are doing, and reach for quality.

6. *Do everything in spiritual growth teams!*

Invite people into spiritual growth through worship leadership—do not recruit people to do a task because they happen to have some expertise. The latter will burn out and leave you in the midst of incomplete change. More than this, only when worship change is clearly and excitedly anchored in spiritual growth does it have credibility in the church. Encourage your leaders to talk openly about the joy of their own growth, not just the importance of a job.

7. *Add on, let go, and never go backward!*

Assure traditional veterans that you will not take away "their" worship service. On the other hand, when these same veterans become receptive to change, do not hesitate to do it. Uniformity is what you are letting go.

Different people need different worship opportunities. A variety of worship services will come and go, but never go back on the principles of diversity and quality. Multiply and upgrade!

No matter how successful these coaching strategies may be, worship change will still be stressful. The core value you must defend is not harmony but growth.

Earlier, I used the evolution of golf to illustrate the impact of technology on sports. The manner in which coaches for change introduce and use technology, however, is equally significant. Imagine the scandal and controversy surrounding J. H. Taylor innovating his way around the Prestwick golf course in 1893 through this eyewitness account:

> In his ignorance of precept and tradition he thought not of [the past]. "Excelsior" was his motto, and he played at the hole with putter, iron, and driver with the same determination and *sang-froid*. And the manner in which he placed his full iron and brassey shots was a revelation to all.... He had unconsciously realized the possibilities of the game with the short headed clubs, and not being bound down by any traditions, had been able to work out his own salvation... which culminated in his winning the championship later on.[3]

A similar spirit, I suspect, motivates the technological innovators of the postmodern church. The key is not that they disdain the past, but that they are so passionate about Christ's mission into the future. It is a faithfulness that will be a revelation to all.

Notes

1. "Through the 'Green' with the Iron Clubs," in *Golf: A Turn-of-the Century Treasury*, ed. Mel Shapiro, Warren Dohn, Leonard Berger (Secaucus, N.J.: Castle Books, 1986), pp. 271, 273. (Originally published in *Outing* magazine, June 1899.)

2. The folk religion of the Bronze Age celebrated the hearth snake as a protector of the home, and was associated with the earth goddess and agriculture. As men traveled further afield in the Iron Age for trade and war, religious metaphors also shifted to thunderbolts and waterspouts.

3. "Why Golf Has Improved," in *Golf: A Turn-of-the-Century Treasury*, p. 136. (Originally published by Harold Hilton, 1903.)

Chapter Seven

Team Spirit

> In order to build team spirit, transform worship.

Great coaches never underestimate the importance of morale—*esprit de corps*—or team spirit. Team spirit is a fluid that fills the gaps between plays, innings, quarters, halves, substitutions, and line changes to create a great game. It is the bond that joins a string of tragic or glorious individual efforts into a shared experience. Team spirit inspires self-sacrifice and injects hope in the midst of despair. It motivates players to fulfill themselves and surpass themselves in the same moment. It motivates the coaches to be more creative and innovative than during the last game. It motivates the fans to believe in the impossible.

The significance of team spirit in professional sports is often hidden from view. Television commercials or the meaningless banter of commentators have generally usurped the "gaps" in the action where team spirit was most obvious. Occasional views of cheerleaders, marching bands, and mascots are all we see. We do not usually see the celebration, commiseration, or encouragement happening in the locker room or on the sidelines.

The significance of team spirit is more apparent in amateur sports. Indeed, since amateur sports are notoriously short on staffing and insufficiently funded for up-to-date equipment, team spirit may be their most important leverage point for change! There is probably no experience of pandemonium and euphoria like a high school basketball game. I remember playing in the small jazz band that could send both players and fans into a veritable fever of effort. We created an identity bordering on the cultic and a hope bordering on the fanatic.

This context or environment of team spirit is the foundation for leveraging change in the church. You may have the fulcrum, the bar, and the counterbalance all in place, but unless you set the apparatus up in the right context, the whole effort will collapse. No auto mechanic would try to change a tire by placing the jack on soft sand. You have to choose the right foundation, the right context, if the whole effort is to succeed. Study the ground. Test the soil. Look for instabilities in the pavement. Then set the jack and start pumping.

Most coaches of change in the church rightly perceive that *worship* is the foundation on which leverage must rest. It establishes and nurtures the team spirit that unites and motivates the team. One can experiment with everything else in the church, but unless worship begins to be transformed, all experiments will come to nothing. A church can be understaffed and poor, yet birth and nurture a team spirit through transformed worship that can overcome all obstacles.

The crucial importance of worship to facilitate or block change is the reason that worship, among all the stresses of change in the church, is the most volatile. More churches split, more laity depart in anger, and more clergy are driven to disability because of tension over worship than over any other aspect of congregational life. It is not the *style* of worship that is the issue. It is the *purpose* of worship that is controversial. Modern churches mistakenly believe the purpose of worship is:

- *Education.* Worship is the only adult education moment in the week, and therefore it must be packed with all the vital theological and institutional information the denomination thinks the membership needs to know.

- *Remembrance.* Worship is the routine act of preserving a heritage through historic liturgies, cyclical Bible readings, and prayers.

- *Socialization.* Worship is the weekly training experience for families and friends to interact in healthy ways and for children to understand the importance of religion.

Modern church leaders often argue that the purpose of worship is to glorify God. In fact, the purpose of worship is to glorify God by educating, remembering, and socializing around the ecclesiastical heritage of the church.

Postmodern coaches understand that the purpose of worship is to create, build, or nurture team spirit. They, too, believe that the purpose of worship is to glorify God, but they understand that the best way God can be glorified is through motivating God's people to participate in God's mission of redemption. This is not an ecclesiastical issue. It is a mission issue. Worship is about mission. Birthing and nurturing team spirit is not about the preservation of a historic identity but about the advancement of God's realm. If there is a game to be won, it is God's global game to transform the world in the image of Christ.

Coaches for change may not begin church transformation by reorienting worship to nurture team spirit. Indeed, the significance of this in professional religion may have been hidden by the frequent ecclesiastical commercials for generic mission funds and committee recruitment. It may well be easier and more opportune to begin with adult faith formation, the introduction of new technologies, or the training of core leaders in a counterbalanced faith. Inevitably, however, coaches for change must turn their attention to worship. Success in bringing change to worship will usually be the turning point from anxiety to celebration in the transformation of congregational life. It will be achieved at a cost. Worship is the foundation for leverage.

Transforming Worship

There are innumerable worship resources available to help coaches develop new tactics. Coaches can experiment with alternate liturgies, technologies, floor plans, preaching styles, musical forms, and dramatic and visual displays. Read them. Use them. Take what works, discard what does not—and make sure you really know the difference.

It is that final word of caution that is the real crux

> **The Myths Behind Modern Worship**
>
> ❖ The Myth of Reasonable Religion
>
> ❖ The Myth of the Controllable Holy
>
> ❖ The Myth of Progressive Justice
>
> ❖ The Myth of Therapeutic Process
>
> ❖ The Myth of Heavenly Favors

for coaching change in worship. In all the fire and fury of worship experimentation, too many leaders fail to discern the hidden cultural disjunction that lies behind postmodern worship. They mistakenly use options they think will work but fail to leverage the change they want. They mistakenly discard options that they believe "will never work *here*" when it is precisely that challenge that they need to undertake.

There are hidden, uncritically accepted assumptions that lie behind modern worship that must be addressed before any particular tactic for change can be deployed or discarded. These assumptions subtly and decisively shaped the worship patterns of European and North American churches during the last several centuries. With the collapse of Christendom, these assumptions have now become mythologies that are deeply embedded in modern church experience, and these mythologies must be shattered before any tactic for worship change can be truly effective.

The best coaches do not just introduce new tactics. They shatter the old mythologies so the new tactics they introduce have a chance to succeed.

❖ The Myth of Reasonable Religion

Modern people believe in the reasonableness of religion. Deep in their hearts, they believe if only everyone could read and write, the logic of grammar and syntax alone would lead the full diversity of the public to a common agreement. If only everyone could discuss issues calmly over a potluck supper in the church basement, every problem could be negotiated and every conflict could be resolved. If only people were more literate and articulate, every question could be answered. Modern preachers and congregations believe that truth can be summarized, communicated, and understood if only a professional wordsmith or learned committee could find the right words.

Modern worship has become increasingly wordy in an era when the average attention span of adults has been shrinking dramatically. The order of service is long, the pages in the printed bulletin multiply, and the required vocabulary is ever more specialized for church insiders. Preachers expect people to listen to long, complex sentences and appreciate finely phrased rhetoric. They even offer instructions to the uninitiated so that they can become more literate during the act of worship. The wordiness of worship encourages wordy meetings, wordy stewardship campaigns, wordy job descriptions, wordy committee mandates, and wordy mission statements.

Postmodern people believe in the unreasonableness of religion. It is a matter of the heart rather than the mind. Postmodern people probably spend more time than their modern counterparts thinking about faith but without rationalizing faith. They probably spend more time discussing faith but without expecting to arrive at unanimous agreement.

▲ *Faith is an emotionally charged disposition.* Postmodern people are not calm, objective, or detached about their faith. They are emotional, interactive, and connected. They throw themselves into conversation and debate to achieve highly pragmatic goals of mission.

▲ *Truth exceeds all efforts to define it.* Postmodern people are always looking for a new metaphor, image, and experience. When it comes to religion, mere words are never enough. The moment after an experience is described, the description becomes inadequate to convey the experience.

The myth of reasonable religion is shattered by cultural diversity and extreme life experience. This means, whatever worship tactic is deployed or discarded at any given time, postmodern worship will display these characteristics:

1. *Worship is a dialogue of passion.* It incorporates and inspires intense conversation. Participants push their reading glasses up onto their foreheads and start talking to one another. Preachers take questions. Prayer pools expectations. Participants de-

brief about their experiences. The point of worship is not to make people biblically *literate*, but to make them biblically *conversant*.

2. *Worship is a multimedia experience.* It communicates truth in a hundred inadequate ways simultaneously and coaches participants to synthesize it for themselves. People hear the gospel, see images, touch reality, smell the aroma of Christ, and exclaim their response.

Worship is no longer a retreat from the world; it is a discovery of God in the world.

❖ The Myth of the Controllable Holy

Modern people believe they can control grace. Deep in their hearts, they believe if people get a good education and improve themselves, the blessings of God can be predictable and manageable. If people read the right books, obtain the appropriate training, learn the proper skills, assemble the correct facts, and put the puzzle of life together, all will be well. Of course unexpected tragedies and surprising blessings will happen from time to time, but such experiences can be assimilated into the rhythms of an increasingly mobile living. Modern people believe they can regulate how much pain they will tolerate, how much joy they will risk, and how much change they will accept.

Modern worship has become soothing and predictable. The order of "good" worship is eternally the same. The progress of the Christian year may be unintelligible to most participants, but at least one can always anticipate the content of the next committee agenda. Even the lectionary readings are known three years in advance—lest the theme of the message be unduly startling. Denominational standardization assures modern people that the congregation down the street or across the country is doing much the same things. When participants leave, they shake hands politely and either compliment the preacher on the sermon or criticize the worship leader for losing control of the children's story.

Postmodern people believe that grace is essentially, frighteningly uncontrollable. They have learned to live one day at a time because comfortable repetitiveness lulls people into self-destructive addictions. Both the daily agenda and the multiyear strategic plan are continually interrupted by unanticipated experiences.

▲ *Grace explodes all efforts to contain it.* Postmodern people have grown accustomed to sudden changes in career, relationship, and self-awareness. The best things in life are undeserved. Grace is always less than you wanted and more than you can handle, and it carries you away where you did not know you wanted to go.

▲ *Grace is the only truly healthy habit.* Postmodern people treat every discipline, tradition, and pattern with suspicion. The healthiest habit can all too easily become obsession. The happiest relationship can become entrapment. The only safe dependency is God.

The myth of controllability is shattered by gratuitous evil and undeserved grace. This means, whatever worship tactic is deployed or discarded at any given time, postmodern worship will display these characteristics:

3. *Worship simultaneously employs and shatters all cultural forms.* It is an environment in which the unexpected is welcome. Leaders choreograph in detail but are experts at improvisation. Patterns, symbols, and musical styles, no matter how traditional or how contemporary, cannot be repeated forever. The point of worship is not that it is timeless but that it is timely.

4. *Worship is the one habit that breaks all addictions.*
    Daily lifestyle will be shaped around it. It is as
    essential to the week as weight-watching and
    twelve-step programs. It may rarely be pre-
    dictable, but it will never be missed.

If worship is anything less than a necessity for daily living, it is expendable from weekly planning.

❖ The Myth of Progressive Justice

Modern people believe in the virtue of progress. Deep
in their hearts, they believe if only people will be patient,
diligent, and loyal, justice will eventually be served, and
science will eventually guarantee security. The system,
however flawed, is fixable. All we need to create are the
right tools; all we need to fund is the right research and
development strategy; all we need to develop are the
right skills; all we need to legislate are the right laws.
Modern people believe that one day—somehow, somewhere—someone will cure all diseases, right all wrongs,
balance all the books, and guarantee tomorrow will be
OK. Just wait.

Modern worship has become passive. It encourages
participants to trust authoritative denominational offices
and invest in generic mission funds. It does not motivate
mission but motivates certification so an approved few
can do mission and everyone else will pray for them.
Modern worship places people into committees of the
churched rather than sending them into mobs of the
unchurched. It calms people, puts events into historic
perspective, and bids participants to think about it some
more before doing anything precipitate. Time is on our
side.

Postmodern people believe in intervention. They
sense that time is running out, and the situation is
urgent. Things may be better or worse than they were,
but it is not inevitably so.

▲ *Justice is a personal choice that can always be avoided.* Postmodern people make justice a matter of personal decision rather than institutional mandate. Their questions are not How shall I vote? or Whom shall we send? but What can I do? and Where should I go?

▲ *Security is the serene acceptance of ambiguity.* Postmodern people accept a fundamental *yes* and *no* in daily living. Choices are rarely black and white. The only security lies in preparedness, not safety nets.

The myth of progressive justice is shattered by political scandal and disillusionment with corporate profiteering. This means, whatever worship tactic is deployed or discarded at any given time, postmodern worship will display these characteristics:

5. *Worship motivates risky missions.* It inspires participants to make their own lives more vulnerable to change for the sake of a higher purpose. It sends them to intervene in situations of crisis. The point of worship is not a tax benefit, but a life benefit.

6. *Worship is an act of moral courage.* It calls participants to accept direct ownership for God's world. Acceptance of ambiguity actually empowers action because the need to wait for certainty is removed. The courage of the postmodern Christian is not to do what is *certainly* right, but to do what is *probably* right.

Worship is the method impatient people use to direct their interventions and measure their risks.

❖ **The Myth of Therapeutic Process**
Modern people believe in therapy. Deep in their hearts, they believe if only people could find the right healing technique, aromatherapy, chiropractic manipulation,

exercise program, diet regimen, medical treatment, or marriage retreat, they would be able to love themselves, their intimate partners, and the world. If only people could find the right psychoanalyst or the affordable counselor or the truly sensitive pastor who would visit constantly and preach illuminating sermons about the inner psyche, they would love God more. Modern people believe there really is a book to read, a process to engage, or a website to visit that will finally deal with their issues about divorce, singleness, office alienation, sibling rivalry, generation gaps, and personal insecurity, freeing them to find sexual, emotional, and relational fulfill- ment—if only they could find the resource.

Modern worship has been reduced to mere pastoral care. It is designed to attract needy, unhealthy people with low self-esteem who want experts to take care of them. Healthy people now stay away from church wor- ship in the same way that they avoid hospital emergency rooms and unemployment lines. They will go if they must, but they do not want to do it. The liturgies are depressing, the preaching is condescending, and the people tend to be preoccupied with their own shortcom- ings—whatever those might be. The order of service prays for needy church members, laments the collapse of social safety nets, promises visitation from the staff, and advertises programs to remedy personal complaints. The offering has become a monthly subscription to a dubious therapeutic technique that is not really respected by medical professionals.

Postmodern people believe that authentic love is a state of perpetual jeopardy. They do not wait for the cul- mination of a happy therapeutic process before risking intimate relationships. They leap into harm's way.

▲ *Love is a discovery to be cherished.* Postmodern people find love by accident, and when they have found it, they surrender all they have to keep it. It is not something they deserve that has been denied and can be obtained again with the help of a therapeutic process. It is an unexpected, beautiful mystery found in the very context of personal struggle and ambiguity.

▲ *Intimacy is too fragile for human hands.* Postmodern people have seen their parents work ever harder at intimacy, fail, and fall apart. They recognize that human hands are essentially too clumsy for such a delicate experience. It must be entrusted to a larger, shared spirituality.

The myth of therapeutic process is shattered by well-intentioned, broken marriages and by chronically abusive, dependent relationships. This means, whatever worship tactic is deployed or discarded at any given time, postmodern worship will display these characteristics:

7. *Worship builds radical trust.* It guides participants into a covenant, not a therapy. Love becomes a leap, a risk, a commitment, a decision in which there are no guarantees. It does not lead people back into themselves to ponder their shortcomings, but it guides them beyond themselves to ponder the potential of their Beloved.

8. *Worship creates intimacy with Jesus.* It creates a larger context of intimacy with God that envelops the fragility of all other loving relationships. Love with God and love with cherished human beings are one passion. The abstraction of God's love is enfleshed, and the carnality of human affection is ennobled.

Worship is the celebration of incarnate love placed in constant risk.

❖ The Myth of Heavenly Favors

Modern people believe that good fortune can be purchased by obedience. Deep in their hearts, they believe that good luck is a selling point for faith. If only people would subscribe to the Protestant work ethic, translate the Ten Commandments into civic responsibility, pray regularly, attend church services monthly, and visit their aging parents in the nursing home occasionally, they would be more likely to have better health, fewer crises, and win the lottery. Good things come to those people who lead good lives. This myth is not new to the modern world, but modern people have given it a new twist. Just be sure to publish a line in the local newspaper's "personals" to give thanks to St. Jude or the Holy Spirit for favors received.

Modern worship has become an investment to underwrite the future. Grandparents attend so their grandchildren will learn to perpetuate the institution. Parents bring their children so the kids will obtain the Christian foundation for a successful life. Participants regularly thank God that they are better off than so many others. The primary reason members drop out is that they cannot understand why God has allowed something really bad to happen to them (good people that they are). This distortion of worship is not new in the history of the church, but modern people have given it a new twist. Indulgences have been replaced by indulgent clergy. Postmodern people believe in being tenaciously hopeful. They hope for the best, without really knowing what it will look like and without any collateral with which to borrow it.

▲ *Hope is a fearless connection with God.* Postmodern people seek a rapport of shared meaning that is the one constant amid both good and bad luck. It is a relationship, not an answer. It is an ongoing experience of benevolence, not a rare lottery jackpot.

▲ *Hope is a confidence in divine inevitability.* Postmodern people are convinced that for every person, and for society as a whole, there will be a time of reckoning—sometime, somehow. The context of this time may be ecological, political, economic, or cultural, but it will be unavoidable and transformational. Things *will* be different!

The myth of heavenly favors is shattered by undeserved disappointment and impersonal victimization. This means, whatever worship tactic is deployed or discarded at any given time, postmodern worship will display these characteristics:

9. *Worship is an extremely* enjoyable *experience.* It elicits joy from the participants. It is a pleasure to attend. People are glad to participate. The music and message, images and prayers, style and structure are all familiar, relevant, and engrossing.

10. *Worship is an extremely* unsettling *experience.* It disturbs participants in profound ways. It forces them to consider changing life priorities. It pushes them to reconsider past assumptions. It sends them into reality to test new ideas. The message and mission, the covenant and calling are ambitious, practical, and compelling.

Worship is extreme. It does not politely pass the peace and make people smile. It aggressively proclaims a vision and stirs people to laughter and tears. It is both a joy and a shock at the same time.

The Focus of Stress

Coaches understand that building authentic team spirit may well be the most difficult thing to accomplish.

You can refocus leadership, develop players, and prepare for contemporary mission; but unless a fresh spirit captures the church, all these advances will be frustrated. Worship is the crucible of team spirit. It is in worship that the identity of the church—its core values, bedrock beliefs, motivating vision, and key mission—is revealed and proclaimed.

If coaching were a science, then coaches could follow a blueprint of tactics to transform the church. Coaching, however, is an art. In order to transform worship, one must go deeper to uncover the hidden assumptions that shape congregational identity and limit mission. You must shatter the mythologies of the modern world that have entrapped worship. In the eyes of postmodern people, the "good" worship modern people defend is, in fact, addicted to unhealthy modern perspectives that are foreign to the gospel.

Use any tactic that works. Change the music, introduce drama, multiply volunteer leadership, or modify the method to deliver the message. Use "blended" worship or "multitracked" worship. Do whatever seems to be most opportune and least stressful. But never deceive yourself into thinking there will not come a decisive moment of crisis. Eventually, it will come. There will be a confrontation of spirits. If you have counterbalanced your leaders, matured your players, and equipped for the modern mission field, this crisis can be overcome in a healthy and positive manner. You may lose a few members, but the majority of growing Christian participants will be more enthusiastic and even the angels will sing.

Do not compromise. In the end, a church can have multiple options in style and purpose. You can even have very "traditional" worship services among other options. Great coaches know, however, that despite multiple lines within the team, *there can be only one team spirit.*

Leveraging Change

The diagram below summarizes the steps coaches take to leverage change in the church. Assemble all the pieces:

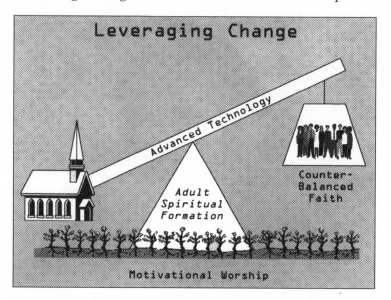

Counterbalance the faith of core leaders. Prepare them in advance for the effort it will take to bear down on the lever.

Establish the fulcrum of adult spiritual formation. Engage adult congregational participants in disciplines of spiritual growth.

Position the lever of technological advance. Upgrade technology in worship and all aspects of congregational life to empower new perspectives on life and mission.

Place the entire apparatus on a foundation of positive team spirit. Transform worship options to motivate mission and build consensus around team identity and purpose.

Now prepare yourself to motivate continuous effort to grow, change, and risk mission for years to come.

Coach of
the Year!

The primary unit of measurement for a coach is the season. Players celebrate a swing, an inning, a play, and a game. Coaches think long term. It may take several seasons of experimentation and team building to finally succeed.

- No great college football coach has won a bowl game on his first endeavor.
- Few professional hockey teams win the Stanley Cup on the first attempt.
- Great baseball teams win many pennants but rarely play the World Series.
- Amateur soccer coaches watch kids grow to adulthood on the team without ever winning a trophy.

Great coaches will celebrate winning a championship, but the next day they are back in the arena and locker room casting an even bigger vision, teaching the fundamentals of the game, and courageously making new changes for the next season.

The same long-term thinking is true for other kinds of coaching. Great teachers are usually controversial and fail to gain much recognition in their first years. Great jazz musicians are usually discounted as eccentric and live on bread and water for years before burning their first CD. Great pastors are usually denominational pariahs for years before any of their colleagues ask them for advice.

The reason long-term pastorates are now commonly seen as crucial for church transformation is that the transition to the postmodern world requires long-term coaching. Every context is an original, and every team is unique. Team owners just do not hire a new coach and expect an automatic championship. Every coach needs to stick to the task, endure the catcalls from the fans, survive the jibes from colleagues at the head office, overcome inevitable losses, and take extraordinary risks.

Then, eventually, the team comes together and you experience victorious seasons in the mission field.

Great coaches do not waste their time gloating over former detractors or venting hurt feelings. They are all too aware that, in the end, it was the Lord's doing—not their own. Besides, they are already concentrating on building the team even stronger for the next season.

Chapter Eight

Building Momentum

> Seize the moment!
> Great coaches follow
> every survived
> crisis with another
> daring move.

Momentum is not easy to define, but it is so significant that it is mentioned in almost every team sport. One team has dominated another and seems to have clinched the match. One goal, run, or point after another indicates certain victory. Suddenly, the other team catches fire. Everything that previously missed by a fraction goes in now. The plays that previously did not work gain long yardage. The strategy that did not work in the first six innings suddenly brings a player home. The fans get back into the game. One commentator turns to another and says, "Do you see how the momentum has shifted?"

The importance of momentum is probably more visible in amateur sports because team spirit carries greater weight than professional skills. Compare college football to professional football. College scoring can be remarkably unbalanced and a sudden surge by the underdog in the second half can lead to dramatic come-from-behind wins. The motivation of a coach, the poise and maturity of key players, and a sudden rush of adrenaline can make all the difference.

Momentum almost always shifts just after a major

crisis. Observe how often a fumble recovery, a missed field goal, or an intercepted pass can transform seemingly inevitable defeat into unexpected victory. The team pressed to its own one-yard line recovers the ball. They march down the field and score. Suddenly, it is like a different, fresher, more talented team has taken the field, yet it is the same team.

Momentum is equally significant to bringing change to the church. The shift usually begins with a crisis. Good coaches see in every crisis an opportunity to reverse the momentum of the game. The crisis may emerge anywhere—as leadership becomes counterbalanced, players painfully mature, or technology advances—but it frequently happens in the context of worship. This is the crucible of team spirit. In the church, what is important is not whether you win or lose a particular argument. It is how you coach your key players through the crisis.

Poor coaches:
- finish construction of the new sanctuary, then relax and return to old worship patterns and musical styles;
- lose a particular point of mission strategy with the board, then make ultimatums about leaving;
- establish another new worship alternative and expect the targeted worship participants to connect with all the old cell groups.

Great coaches:
- finish a capital building campaign and immediately press on to create an entirely new mission with the building;
- lose a point of mission strategy, model team cooperation, and immediately communicate one-to-one with core leaders to go deeper into the vision and mission of the church;
- establish a new worship alternative and immediately birth a whole new set of spiritual growth options through the week.

Great coaches do not merely survive or overcome a crisis. They immediately build momentum to win the game. In college football, the first play after a crisis is usually a daring, deep pass to the opposite goal line, and it often works. Seizing the moment, they capitalize on the fire that has newly caught the exhausted team. In the same way, great coaches in the church follow every survived crisis with a daring move.

The Vehicles of Credible Communication

When the crisis occurs and is overcome, a whole new set of communication vehicles emerges in the team—or in the congregation. On the sports field, you not only see the coach in constant movement and conversation along the sidelines and over the microphone, but you also see the players moving and talking among themselves. There is a sudden animation of verbal and nonverbal communication. Too many traditional pastors not familiar with the coaching role fall back into habits that actually block or decelerate momentum.

Bad Coaching	Great Coaching
Preacher to Congregation	Friend to Friend
Clergy to Laity	Team to Team
CEO to Stockholders	Explorer to Spiritual Travelers
Senior Pastor to Associates	Mentor to Apprentices
Denominational Authority to Personnel Committee	Visionary to Core Leaders
Pastor to Dissidents	Triad to Dissidents

Great coaches follow up crisis by shifting their communication from strategic control to spiritual influence. The truth is, management can still be entrusted to others. What they need is the visionary influence of a coach who can anticipate future complexities and discern what the end of the game might look like.

Friend to Friend

The most potent force to build momentum is not the coach haranguing the team in the locker room (or from the pulpit); it is the coach who motivates the players to talk among themselves. Few sermons, no matter how rhetorically masterful they might be, are memorable enough to motivate postmodern people. It is the friendly conversation between congregational friends in the coffee shop and over the telephone that goes furthest to persuade, encourage, exhort, and create unity. When a great coach sees a player who is resentful, bewildered, or confused, he or she does *not* talk to the player personally. He or she sends one of the player's friends—one who is enthusiastic and can talk intimately and nonconfrontationally with the other.

Team to Team

Great coaches do not pull rank, presume upon entitlements, call people into their office, or deliver strategic commands. They speak as a team to a team. In large organizations, it may be the coaching and training staff addressing the different lines of players. In a small organization, it may be the coach and key players talking to the team as a whole. Do not dress up in your cassock alb, don your clerical collar, or call church members into your office to address them beneath your Doctor of Ministry certificate mounted on the wall. Gather your colleagues or core leaders and, together, address the membership. Do it informally and in their natural life context. Do it as one united team—each member with a unique role or position to play, and each person prepared to hear the advice of the other.

Explorer to Spiritual Traveler

Traditional church leaders (particularly in large congregational organizations) have the habit of addressing the church as a CEO might speak to stockholders. It perpetuates the illusion that strategic planning and management lie in their hands, and the people of God are fund-raisers who hold the staff accountable for their investment. Traditional leaders approach an annual congregational meeting with a "state of the union" speech and a five-year plan. Great coaches do nothing of the sort. They come to the congregation in buckskins and boots, fresh from the mission field, equipped with hard data and intuitive perception, ready to identify emerging opportunities, dangerous pitfalls, and alternative routes through the cultural wilderness. They are explorers pointing the way to fellow travelers. Together they weigh the risks, recognize the ambiguities, and accept the dangers.

Mentor to Apprentices

The hierarchical world of Christendom in which the senior pastor with the largest income told the associate staff what to do is gone. The postmodern game is much too fast paced to allow that to continue. Notice how head coaches of major sports teams give coaching and training staff, quarterbacks and team captains enormous autonomy to discern, design, and implement strategy. Great coaches establish a trusted, mentoring relationship with staff and core congregational leaders that rarely (*very* rarely) involves management. They comment, critique, suggest, affirm, warn, or encourage their partners. Occasionally, they receive the same treatment. Their goal is not to control the staff in order to win this particular game but to help the staff mature to become great coaches in their own right.

Visionary to Core Leaders

As the modern church collapses into recrimination and litigation, the personnel committee has taken an exaggerated importance in the life of the church. Traditional clergy respond by posing as denominational authorities on polity (affirmatively or critically) and by entering into complex power struggles with personnel committees. Great coaches avoid this. It is a trap that merely entangles them in a dying church system. Instead, they constantly reshape, rethink, review, and rejoice in the vision that motivates everything they seek to do. The vision is primarily articulated among a small group of core congregational leaders (staff and volunteers), who in turn explain it to others in their own way. Vision is the primary vehicle of accountability in the postmodern church, not polity. Great coaches stake their jobs not on their denominational expertise but on the size, character, and inclusiveness of their visions.

Triad to Dissident

The biblical model of sending three credible church leaders to talk with those who are angry, troubled, fractious, or unethical is the best model for the postmodern world as well. Do not send the pastor. A personal visit from the clergy will not solve anything. It will exhaust the clergy, falsely empower the dissident with more leverage over the church, and sideline the congregation as mere observers. Instead, send three of the most credible, spiritual, respected members of the church. Their presence models team spirit, establishes a nonconfrontational environment, and opens the door for the prodigal to return home.

Responding to the Degrees of Control

Coaches seeking to build momentum for congregational change will inevitably meet opposition.

Opposition will always manifest itself in varying degrees of control as individuals or groups try to protect their own domain, limit the advance of the new vision, or undermine emerging leadership. Control is the key obstacle today for effective church transformation.

The following table is a typology of escalating degrees of control. Whether or not momentum continues, great coaches can expect to experience these heightening phases of control. Failure to address the early stages of control allows resistance to change to increase. Speaking in sports metaphor, it is as if the renewed momentum of the team trying to come from behind is slowed down or even reversed. However, success in confronting the early stages of control may also drive resistance to become more desperate. In sports metaphor, it is as if the team trying to stop the come-from-behind momentum starts taking needless penalties for personal fouls and unsportsmanlike conduct. Either way, one builds momentum by countering inevitable and escalating attempts to control the church.[1]

Degree of Control	Coaching Response
Fiefdom and Faction	Organizational Identity and Multiple Options
Denial and Denigration	Mission Awareness and Storytelling
Indecision and Inflexibility	Motivating Vision and Adult Spiritual Formation
Hostage-Taking and King-Making	Risky Commitment and Authentic Leadership

The goal of great coaching is not to take away power but to transform dysfunctional control into shared responsibility. Dysfunctional control manipulates organizational life to assuage personal fears or balance individual insecurities. "The church will be the rock of my existence!" Shared responsibility frees organizational life to fulfill the purpose of God and the mission of the team. "The church will be the environment in which we can fulfill our calling!" Building momentum for change does not require a struggle to *hold* power but a struggle to *focus* power.

Fiefdom and Faction

These two forms of control are actually very similar. The one leads inevitably to the other. Consider the following signals that this type of control is emerging to slow the momentum of change:

- *I'm the organist here, and I control the music program!*

- *You may want it, but it's the Lifetime Trustees who will decide!*

- *Let's rally the Supper Club and get a petition against this idea!*

- *I'll come to church, but I will withhold my offering envelopes!*

The desire to stake out one's own territory and protect one's dominance over a limited program area leads inevitably to a more aggressive behavior against change. Offense is always the best defense.

Great coaches recognize that this is an issue not of authority but of identity. Therefore, it will not be resolved by committees learning polity or by appeals to the bishop for clarity. The question to be answered is not "Who is in charge?" but "Who are we?" The emergence of fiefdom and faction leads coaches back to the clear articulation of shared values and beliefs. Clarity and ownership of identity allows the multiplication of strategic options. The diversity of individuals and groups are assured that there is a place for them in the organization.

Denial and Denigration

The similarity of these two forms of control is that they are attempts to perpetuate an organizational self-image that no longer connects with reality. Consider the following signals that this form of control is emerging to slow the momentum of change:

➥ *What problem? I don't see a problem with this church!*

➥ *But my daughter likes it here, and she's a teenager!*

➥ *Those people think they're just so much better than the rest of us!*

➥ *If the public weren't such sinners, they would come to church!*

➥ *The pastor is a tyrant!*

Controllers choose inaction based on limited or distorted information. Life is always more wonderful inside the church than it really is, and life is always more frightening in the world than it really is. Controllers believe the integrity of people who question either assumption must be attacked. The accusations of elitism or tyranny in others is merely a reflection of the accuser's judgmentalism.

Great coaches recognize that this is not an issue of personality but the perception of reality. Therefore, it will not be resolved by Myers-Briggs personality inventories or youth representation in committees. The question to answer is not "Who is right?" but "What is our network?" The emergence of denial and denigration leads coaches to do serious and extensive demographic research, deploy listeners to dialogue with the community, engage consultants to assess congregational life, and establish global partners in conversation about faith and witness. They are not satisfied with reporting data. They multiply storytelling by allowing more and more voices within the church to share their spiritual growth and mission consciousness.

Indecision and Inflexibility

It may seem surprising to connect seemingly pointless organizational dithering with aggressive theological dogmatism or procedural legalism, but these controlling behaviors spring from the same source. When controllers want to slow or stop momentum, they trap the energies of the church in structure. Consider the following signals that this type of control is emerging to slow the momentum of change:

➼ *Let's form an ad hoc committee and think about this again!*

➼ *Wait! My minority group hasn't filed a report yet!*

➼ *Paragraph 6 of section 15 in the denominational polity requires ... !*

➼ *Christian orthodoxy forbids it!*

This indecision or inflexibility is not just fear of making a mistake but fear of making a choice. Once a decision is made of any kind, power is surrendered. Controllers may make the criteria for making a decision so restrictive that nothing can be done; or they may make the criteria so dependent on their personal views that nothing can be done. Micromanagement and macrogeneralization achieve the same goal. Both controlling behaviors appeal to integrity, thus implying that any risk, experiment, or alternative interpretation of faith must be inherently reckless.

Great coaches recognize that behavior is an issue of spirituality, not management. Therefore, it will not be resolved by voting procedures, board restructuring, or intervention by the denominational office. The question is not "What assurances do we have that this is the right strategy?" but "What confidence do we have that this is the right direction?" The emergence of indecision and inflexibility causes coaches to rearticulate vision, establish organizational boundaries, and create systems to learn from mistakes. They guide board members away from management toward adult spiritual formation.

Hostage-Taking and King-Making

Hostage-taking and king-making are much the same thing, except that the hostage in the latter case is the pastor. Both behavior patterns demand that team spirit itself be sacrificed in the name of diplomacy.

Hostage-taking is the desperate action of controllers who threaten to harm all or part of the congregational team if their demands are not met. Consider the following signals:

• *My family and I are leaving, and you will never see our children in Sunday school again!*

• *If you do this, the choir (or Sunday school teachers or finance committee or whoever) will resign!*

As in all hostage situations, there can be no compromise. The situation might be defused to become a factional fight (as in the first degree of control) and be remedied by a celebration of organizational identity and multiple options. By this time, however, the issue is usually not about identity and options but about dominance. It is the source, not the size, of the vision that is at stake. Will identity emerge from the spiritual growth of the people, or will it be imposed by a small group of the oldest or boldest members? Compromise here will shatter team spirit altogether. Better that a few leave so spirituality can grow unrestrained and creative. The church can overcome a financial crisis if vision emerges from below, but it will never survive even the smallest crisis if vision is imposed from above.

King-making is actually the more insidious and dangerous controlling behavior because it appeals to the egos of church leaders. Large churches can build enormous momentum, grow to include huge memberships, and multiply many ministries but ultimately be caught in the trap of this controlling behavior. Consider the following signals:

- *You can be the pastor, Reverend, if I can be your right-hand man!*

- *How will our group choose a worthy successor when our pastor retires?*

It is the pastor who becomes the hostage. His or her leadership is indebted to the patronage of a few influential people. His or her creativity is limited by the permission of an influential few. The pastor can become an enormous success but only if programs and ministries are approved by a *de facto* board that lies hidden in the shadows. Ultimately, such patronage cripples leadership and shatters team spirit.

Great coaches recognize that these are issues of authenticity, not diplomacy. Therefore, they cannot be resolved by budget negotiation about programs or by political appointments to key ministries. There are no deals. Ministries must happen because the Spirit elicits them from the spiritual depths of the people. Ministry leadership must be appointed because individuals are gifted and called to the work of God. The coach must earn credibility by the authenticity of his or her own spiritual life and calling or surrender leadership to another.

Do You Have What It Takes to Be a Coach?

Not every player can be a coach. Star players can occasionally inspire their teammates, train rookies, and equip a team, but in the long run they cannot rebuild a team and win the pennant. Not every traditionally trained minister can coach a postmodern church. Successful denominational pastors can occasionally erect a new church building, train apprentice preachers, and mobilize volunteer programs, but in the long run they cannot rebuild a team that thrives in the postmodern world. The real test comes when leaders try to sustain momentum for change because when it comes to building momentum, great coaches are a different kind of leader.

❖ *Great coaches are* honest, *not merciful*. Unlike most modern church pastors, who were born with tender hearts, raised to be kind to everyone, and trained in compassionate pastoral care, postmodern coaches are remarkably hard, candid, and demanding. They are honest with their criticism and with their praise. They rarely leave anyone in doubt about their emotions, preferences, or opinions.

❖ *Great coaches are* intuitive, *not analytical*. Unlike most modern church pastors, who can take a church apart, put it back together blindfolded, and repeat the process anywhere they are appointed or called, postmodern coaches are remarkably limited. Remove them from the synergy of their context and team, and they are nearly helpless in developing a strategic plan. They make a decision because it feels right, take a risk because the time is right, and add new ministries because it just seems to fit.

❖ *Great coaches are* daring, *not cautious*. Unlike most modern church pastors, who do not take chances with their pension plan and never make decisions without universal consultation, postmodern coaches are remarkably audacious. They are prepared to do whatever it takes to achieve the impossible and to accept the responsibility for victory or defeat.

Great coaches will scrap any "sacred cow" without hesitation (be it property, program, or policy) if it is ineffective in building the team or achieving the mission. They will try any radical idea (without denominational permission or universal approval) if it will nurture people and build God's realm. They will take on any project (however costly in heritage, staffing, or money) if it will advance the team toward its vision. Not only will they do this, but the day after victory, they will call the elders of the church into the sanctuary and ask God to help them do it all over again.

Can you be a great coach in the postmodern world? The test comes when you inevitably lose people from the church that you are transforming. Christendom pastors have been raised and trained to feel deep shame if they lose one of their flock. Therefore, they worry that any transformational strategy to leverage change might alienate one of their beloved, veteran members. This fear of losing anybody makes Christendom pastors extraordinarily cautious—too cautious for the postmodern world!

Great coaches know that there are basically three kinds of people in the church at the turn of the millennium.

- First, there is a growing minority who are eager for change to catch up to their workplace, home life, and leisure environments. These people are ready to go.

- Second, there is a large majority of conservative, cautious people who really do not understand change and who are generally afraid of it. Yet these people are nevertheless *healthy* people and can be persuaded, educated, encouraged, mentored, cajoled, and coached. They are at least open to change.

• Finally, there is a small minority of dysfunctional people obsessed with control for its own sake. The Christendom church has magnetically attracted these dysfunctional people by posing as the last bastion of stability in a chaotic world. These people are essentially *unhealthy* people. They are control addicts, and therefore, no amount of persuasion, education, or mentoring will help them. They are virtually *unable* to be open to change.

The first group requires visionary leadership, and the second requires clear training. The third group, however, requires "tough love." Indulgent compassion disguised as pastoral psychotherapy may keep them content for a while, but it will not help them become healthy people, and it will sabotage God's mission for the church.

  If you want to become a great coach in the postmodern world, you have to decide whom you want to lose. Please understand: you no longer have a choice about losing some people! That is the stressful dilemma for traditionally nurtured and trained clergy. You desperately do not want to lost anyone, but at the turn of the millennium, *you no longer have a choice.*

  If you attend to the dysfunctional controllers, you will not only deepen their dysfunctional addictions, but you will lose the growing minority of people who are ready and eager for change. They will not wait for you. They have no confidence that more time or education will help people addicted to control. They will leave. Indeed, they are probably already leaving. Their large numbers will be replaced by a few newcomers who are dysfunctional, unhealthy people looking for an unchanging rock in their existence.

On the other hand, if you respond to the growing minority of people who are ready and eager for change, you will lose that dysfunctional, unhealthy minority who have a need to control or be controlled. Some of them are your best financial contributors since money *is* a primary means of control, and they have long used it effectively to resist change. Many, many newcomers who are healthy people seeking to experience the touch of God, however, will replace their small numbers.

The daunting choice paralyzes many Christendom leaders. It challenged the apostolic leaders of the Jerusalem church in biblical times as well. You simply cannot serve God and mammon at the same time. Either you are committed to mission, or you are committed to maintenance, but it cannot be both. Either fish or cut bait.

Some postmodern leaders will cease being pastors and equip themselves to be challenging therapists, addiction interventionists, and chaplains to the terminally ill. They will not placate the controllers, but they will be willing to invest all of their time with just a handful of people. God bless them! That, too, is a ministry of God. Other postmodern leaders will cease being pastors and become coaches for growing churches that give life and empower mission for both healthily eager and healthily cautious people. They are the postmodern leaders of a new species of growing Christian organizations.

Note

1. I am indebted in the formulation of my typology to Donna J. Markham's excellent book *Spiritlinking Leadership: Working Through Resistance to Organizational Change* (Mahwah, N.J.: Paulist Press, 1999), which she wrote for nonprofit organizations. I have adapted her seven intraorganizational behavior patterns and created eight degrees of control experienced in the changing church. Her original seven are: Isolation, projection, splitting, doing/undoing, denial, rigidity, depression. The rearrangement, redefinition, and additions are mine, but her influence is unmistakable.

Chapter Nine

Courageous Leadership

The shift from vision to action is a natural step to take.
Today that simple, unthinking step has become an act of incredibly audacious courage.

Traditional ecclesiastical leaders take themselves far, *far* too seriously. That is the chief obstacle they face to become great coaches in the postmodern world. A taste of P. G. Wodehouse will illustrate my meaning. Wodehouse wrote a series of humorous stories about golf told by the "Oldest Member" of the club.

The Oldest Member, snug in his favorite chair, had long since succumbed to the drowsy influence of the weather. His eyes were closed, his chin sunk upon his breast.... Suddenly the stillness was broken. There was a sharp, crackling sound as of splitting wood. The Oldest Member sat up blinking. As soon as his eyes had become accustomed to the glare, he perceived that a foursome had holed out on the ninth and was disintegrating. Two of the players were moving with quick, purposeful steps in the direction of the side door which gave entrance to the bar; a third was making for the road that led to the village, bearing himself as one in profound dejection; the fourth came on to the terrace.

"Finished?" said the Oldest Member....

"We won on the last green. Jimmy Fothergill and I were playing the vicar and Rupert Blake."

"What was that sharp, cracking sound I heard?" asked the Oldest Member.

"That was the vicar smashing his putter. Poor old chap, he had rotten luck all the way round, and it didn't seem to make it any better for him that he wasn't able to relieve his feelings in the ordinary way."

"I suspected some such thing," said the Oldest Member, "from the look of his back as he was leaving the green. His walk was the walk of an overwrought soul."[1]

The Oldest Member goes on to speculate whether clergy "should not be more liberally handicapped than the laymen with whom they compete."

If the Oldest Member were part of the church rather than the country club, he or she would have made a significant point. Traditional clergy do tend to be more handicapped in organizational transformation in contrast to the entrepreneurship of their business, education, and nonprofit lay leaders. It is not just that they cannot curse when they make mistakes. The problem is they cannot make mistakes, behave aggressively, or act daringly without incredible guilt and anxiety. Traditional clergy were raised in peace, trained in conflict resolution, and certified to build unity. Their career path cannot tolerate chaos. When modern clergy become post-modern coaches, their walk is the walk of an "overwrought soul."

There are models of great coaching in the diversity and history of the Christian church. They are almost always found in times and places of extraordinary transition. It may be in a transition between cultures or a transition between eras. These transitional moments create a church and social context that is very fluid. All the old principles and certainties vanish. Entrepreneurial spirits write their own rules.

One entrepreneurial spirit wrote what has become known as the Benedictine Rule. Who would have expected to find an example of great coaching that is instructive for the postmodern world in the medieval abbeys of the premodern world? The new rules for church leadership developed by the person or persons later identified as St. Benedict have been described as

- a synthesis of practical wisdom and faith,
- a balance between daily living and eternity,
- a guide to shape an entire lifestyle around spirituality,
- a plan to orient all human activity toward the goal of salvation.

Far from being the oppressive regimen imagined by modern Christians, the new rules of Benedict provided an atmosphere of "prudent leniency"[2] that allowed personal achievement within the boundaries of a close-knit community.

In other words, the sixth century Benedictine Rule that was valued so highly in the chaos following the collapse of the Roman Empire is remarkably similar to the twenty-first century congregational organization emerging from the chaos following the collapse of Christendom. Both eras witness the emergence of new rules for revolutionary times. The details of Benedictine monastic life cannot simply be transposed to postmodern times, but the pattern or principles of coaching *can* be profoundly instructive. As Robert Wuthnow suggests, the Benedictine Rule addresses the same yearning for stability and discovery today as it did then.[3]

If the abbey community resembles a postmodern team, the abbot resembles a postmodern coach. Both community and team thrive in a consensus of behavioral expectations that synthesize daily living and spiritual growth. Both community and team position themselves to simultaneously reach in to the heart of the gospel and reach out to the needs of the world. In the midst of this delicate balance, the abbot and the postmodern coach function in similar ways "to build up the weak and to spur on the spirited."[4]

The new rules of St. Benedict are said to have emerged from his experience of simultaneously valuing the classical learning of his time and being disillusioned by the immorality of his colleagues in the classroom. When he was a promising young student of the *liberalia studia* (grammar, rhetoric, and law), he ran away from the decadence and inwardness of his promising ecclesiastical career. His new rules valued learning but transcended them for the sake of the kingdom of God.[5]

Postmodern coaches share a similar ambivalence toward the profound heritage of their tradition and the inexcusable behavior of their denomination. This is how knowledgeable, yet disillusioned, postmodern coaches view the modern alternatives for religious leadership at the turn of the millennium:

The *seers*, once associated with the evangelical right, are dressed in nonecclesiastical business clothes, affect authoritative titles, and are adept in mass communications. They surround themselves with an air of certitude and dismiss skepticism with a knowing smile. Periodically their eyes glaze and stare into the heavens, then fix the expectant supplicant with a look of steel and pronounce the particular program, policy, or perspective required to avoid economic debacle or spiritual doom.

The *advocates*, once associated with the liberal left, are dressed in casual clothes decorated by historic symbols of Christendom. They affect politically correct inclusive language and are adept in small group communications. They surround themselves with an air of competence and respond to skepticism with demographic statistics. Periodically they quote important books, fix the errant questioner with a look of steel, and pronounce the particular program, policy, or perspective required to avoid nuclear meltdown or spiritual naïveté.

The *institutionalists*, once associated with judicatory leadership for both the right and the left, are dressed in ecclesiastical clothes and lapel pins identifying the favored cause of the moment. They affect theological precision and are adept with church structures and procedures. They surround themselves with an air of authority and answer skepticism by appealing to office, polity, and ethos. Periodically they mention church ancestors, fix the loyal follower with a look of steel, and pronounce the particular program, policy, or perspective required to avoid denominational disharmony or spiritual heresy.

Postmodern church leaders flee promising ecclesiastical careers to formulate new rules for the twenty-first century. None of the previous leadership models makes sense in a transitional era. Too many leaders claim to be servants of a higher power, a higher ethic, or a higher authority; but none of them seems to be a servant of a mysterious God who is simultaneously employing, shaping, and shattering the ecclesiastical structures and culture forms that were once so familiar to us. Whatever the new rules for congregational life and mission might be, three major principles of coaching lie behind them.

Obedience

In the nonhierarchical world of postmodern teams, obedience is given not to an office or an individual but to an overarching *vision.* Great coaches instill, nurture, and encourage that vision, then model, advise, and motivate surrender to it.

Many modern church leaders see visions. Only a few are prepared to surrender to them. That is the difference between commentators calling the play-by-play in the television studio and great coaches yelling, stomping, pleading and planning on the sideline. Both may see a vision, but only the latter is obedient to it.

It is this obedience that is the real heart of the Benedictine Rule. In order to be a true father to the community, the abbot must model what it means to surrender to a greater vision of God. In order to be truly effective, the coach must demonstrate to the team what it means to be obedient to a great purpose.

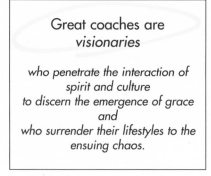

Great coaches are
visionaries

who penetrate the interaction of spirit and culture
to discern the emergence of grace and
who surrender their lifestyles to the ensuing chaos.

These visionaries enable communities of the sixth century or twenty-first century to chart a course between imagination and integrity, risk and recklessness. They thrive in the experience of ambiguity, not the knowledge of absolute certainties. They do not use culture as a neutral stepping-stone to the supernatural nor do they attack culture as an enemy of spirituality. They recognize that culture is the expression of spirit, and spirit is the energy of culture. They discern within the interaction of spirit and culture the signs of hope.

These visionaries—emerging within the former conservative right, liberal left, and institutional center—affect no particular dress or title and have remarkably little professional ambition. They are adept at networking in any media. They surround themselves with an air of radical imagination and common sense and respond to skepticism by a readiness to risk and learn. Repeatedly they articulate single-minded commitment to the gospel, invite spiritual travelers into dialogue, and point toward the path, process, or principle required to facilitate healing and fulfillment.

These types of leaders can coach change in a time of making history. They have no particular personality type and need not excel in any particular professional skill. They may not have any particular educational superiority. Their credibility depends on their own life struggles and spiritual victories, single-minded commitment, openness to share power, and a readiness to learn.

Postmodern coaches can discern the emergence of grace and surrender themselves to the ensuing chaos, because they are obedient to a core process different from the one embodied by the ecclesiastical tradition.

•❖ Christendom institutions assumed the world was a stable, Christian environment that allowed daily life to be predictably shaped around the institutional church. Their core process was the Christian year—with all the feast days, Lenten disciplines, standardized liturgies, common lectionaries, and tidy polities—from the first day of Advent through Christ the King Sunday.

•❖ Post-Christendom leaders recognize that the world is a chaotic, pre-Christian environment in which many gods claim allegiance amid conflicting cultural forms. Their core process is that every day, in every way, every person will be *changed, gifted, called, equipped,* and *sent.*

In the chaos of the twenty-first century, postmodern leaders, like their counterparts in the chaos following the collapse of the Western Roman Empire (and *their* counterparts from the first apostolic age), are obedient to becoming all things to all people, that they might by all means rescue some (see 1 Corinthians 9:22).

It is this audacity to stand on the urban watchtower in order to see a vision that will come in its own time—as well as this intuition to perceive the Kairos moment in the midst of modern culture and this readiness to surrender to the chaos of the infinite simultaneously employs and shatters all cultural forms—that marks the visionary leader. In a sense, great coaches have forsaken the intricacies and idolatries of the Christian year in favor of a single, continuous, explosive, and mysterious *Pentecost* that seizes both a millisecond and the millennium at the same time.

Self-Discipline

Self-discipline provides community or team with whatever stability is possible in a chaotic world. It is a matter of lifestyle, not institutionalization. Benedictine monks took vows of moderation, cooperation, poverty, chastity, and fidelity. Postmodern congregational teams covenant to shape their daily lives around shared core values. The abbot modeled monastic virtues for the community; the coach models the core values of the team. The standards of self-discipline are not the precepts of a denominational personnel policy, but the "Fruits of the Spirit."

Self-discipline is not a welcome word. While vision sounds adventurous and sur-

The Fruits of the Spirit

Love

Joy

Peace

Patience

Kindness

Generosity

Faithfulness

Gentleness

Self-Control

render to vision seems noble, self-discipline feels routine, dull, tedious, and mundane. Yet it is this constant repetition of core values that is the daily task of great coaching. Only when these fundamentals are hammered into the mind and lifestyle of every player, can every player have total confidence in his or her teammates. When the crisis comes in the game (goal line stand, match point, bottom of the ninth with two outs) every player instinctively trusts his or her teammates to behave in an expected way. Building such unthinking trust is the task of coaching.

The most common reason dynamic churches suddenly disintegrate after several seasons of incredible growth and mission is the leaders themselves forget the fundamentals of the game. They stop modeling the core values or spiritual virtues that have been the stable matrix of expectation among congregational participants. One does not need to be moralistic. Every participant—even a pastor—makes mistakes, returns to old addictions, and commits major blunders. Leaders do not model a perfect life; they do model self-criticism. They demonstrate in their daily lifestyle the ability to face responsibility, learn from mistakes, correct behavior, and continuously strive to meet higher standards.

As great coaches make new rules in transitional periods, they remove themselves from external, institutional vehicles of accountability. Therefore, they must commit themselves to internal, congregational vehicles of accountability. The strength of the Benedictine Abbey is the strength of postmodern teams: peer evaluation. If the leader does not share the same discipline as the team, the team disintegrates.

The greatest congregational coaches are hardest on themselves: more rigorous about their own lifestyles, more demanding of their own precious time, and more observant and self-critical of their spontaneous words and deeds. For great coaches

- ▲ their parking space is furthest from the office;
- ▲ their home is closest to the mission field;
- ▲ their day contains the fewest meetings;
- ▲ their routine includes a priority for health;
- ▲ their relational covenants take precedence over career.

The paradox of self-disciplined leadership is that the larger the church becomes, the fewer hours are devoted to management. Such things can be delegated to others. Great postmodern coaches, like Benedictine abbots, concentrate on modeling the vows of community (team) life.

❊ Their commitment to *moderation* reflects their celebration of holistic health, their resistance to work addictions, and their appreciation for personal growth.

❊ Their commitment to *cooperation* reflects their readiness to "let go" of control, honor parallel leadership, and empower team.

❊ Their commitment to *poverty* reflects their priority for relational over material values, renunciation of economic entitlements, and compassion for the oppressed.

❊ Their commitment to *chastity* reflects their single-minded pursuit of God's mission, the simplicity of their lifestyle, and the sincerity of their ministry.

❊ Their commitment to *fidelity* reflects their loyalty to their personal, covenanted relationships to spouse and family.

Great coaches free themselves by such self-discipline to

concentrate on the unfolding vision and its core process, the fundamentals of shared values and their modeling, and the reserves of courage necessary to lead in the post-modern world.

Courage

The greatest terror of authentic spiritual leadership, the nightmare that keeps leaders awake at night, is that people *actually listen* to them! People are actually reshaping their lifestyles, changing their career paths, repriori-tizing their budgets, and redefining their intimate relationships because of the vision that leader has artic-ulated! What if they are wrong? They lie awake at night thinking:

> "What if good people, hungry people, yearn-ing people, *God's people*, change their lifestyles and livelihoods, risk their little babies and eld-erly parents, take themselves to the very edge of risk and ruin only to discover that I am wrong?"

Risking one's own life for a vision is courageous. Risking the lives of others is even more courageous. Shaping ones own lifestyle around a discipline of faith is coura-geous. Risking the livelihoods of others is still more courageous.

> Great coaches know the difference between spiritual authenticity and personal ego.

As important as modeling moral virtues or core values might be, there is a more de-manding self-discipline required of church leaders. They may be grasped by a larger vision and committed to a noble purpose, but they must know the difference between authenticity and ego.

It is instructive for those who work to leverage change in the church to note how often the Bible describes not only the rise of spiritual leaders but also the humbling of spiritual leaders. When Moses, infuriated by the sin of his people, smashed the tablets, his spiritual authenticity crossed the boundary from authenticity to arrogance. Was Moses God—to give, or withhold, the laws of God? Did he perceive the stupidity of the golden calf to be a rejection of God or a betrayal of himself? Having crossed the fine line between authenticity and ego, Moses lost the guardianship of the vision to Joshua.

In the end, Moses would have made a poor abbot and an ineffective coach. Rumi, the thirteenth-century Muslim dervish (perceived by believers and unbelievers alike as simultaneously mystic, monastic, and manic), told a parable that I paraphrase from memory here:

> When Moses journeyed up the mountain to talk to God and receive the tablets of stone, he spied a poor shepherd praying desperately to see God himself. The shepherd was making outlandish promises to curry God's favor. "Appear to me, O God, and I will provide you with a rich tent, I will give you new clothes, I will feed you delicious food, I will comb your hair!" Upon hearing this, Moses was indignant. "God is transcendent, you idiot! How stupid you are trying to win God's favor!" The poor shepherd bowed to Moses' authority and went away very ashamed. Later, when God appeared to Moses to give the commandments, God chastised him. "Today," God said, "you have separated me from one who is searching."

Great coaches do not tell people what to think, but they point people in the right direction to find the answers. This self-restraint is one of the most difficult challenges of leadership.

The end of the millennium has seen the publication of a growing number of bioplanning books written by leaders of large churches. These books offer principles and plans for church growth through the autobiography of the church leader. The birth of a visionary leader is a compelling story, and many of these books offer tremendous insights into church growth in a chaos of cultures. In the pursuit of that vision, however, these leaders too often appear falsely self-deprecating, inflexible over seeming trivialities, and all too ready with ultimatums.

The spiritually hungry, institutionally alienated Christian reader is left with a lingering worry. Has the coach surrendered to a vision or elevated a personal perspective? Has the coach crossed the boundary between vision and arrogance? Is the eccentric behavior, passionate irascibility, "in your face" methodology, and confident risk-taking a sign that Moses is once again leading the Israelites to the Promised Land, or is it a sign that Moses is having a temper tantrum with the tablets of God?

The bioplanning books of successful postmodern apostles—and tragic cult leaders are beginning to look uncomfortably alike. Too often they exhibit a subtle shift from the conviction that God has revealed a vision to the conviction that God has revealed a strategic plan. This is the transition from authenticity to arrogance. It is an escape from moral responsibility. It is the transition from an authentic belief that "It's not me but God working through me!" to the inauthentic arrogance that tacitly communicates, "I am God!"

In the first chapter of this book, I spoke of crossing the boundary between obsessive timidity and radical imagination in the postmodern world. Spiritual coaching that crosses such a boundary is bold. It dares to take risks. ΩIt experiments with seeming impossibilities and synthesizes former polarities. However, just as their congregations live in the tension between timidity and imagination, they also live in a tension between clear vision and strategic ambiguity. The anxious dilemma of coaching is that God reveals what the victory will look like, but God does not provide a game plan with which to achieve it.

Vision is always metaphorical. It is poetry, image, or song, but it is not a plan. The courage of great coaching is in the attempt to make it one. Great coaches spend a lifetime "teasing out" of the metaphor the fullness of God's intention. Is the vision to relieve suffering, make disciples, enrich the poor, free addicts, or bring joy to all?

- What kind of suffering will be relieved?
- What will it mean to be a disciple?
- In what ways will the poor be enriched, and who, in fact, are "the poor"?
- What are the symptoms, and what are the addictions?
- Is it really possible to weep for joy, or can we only joyously weep?

Vision does not answer these questions. The seemingly understandable propositions built into every team mission statement suddenly become mere metaphors, which are only partially clear to the coach.

As clear as coaches may be about vision and as self-disciplined as they may be in pursuing it, they always live in strategic ambiguity. In retrospect, they or their descendants may speak of God telling the leader what to do and how to do it. They may rationalize history by recognizing only a few successes and ignoring the many failed attempts. Everyone remembers a great coach's brilliant plays and tournament triumphs, but few recall the stupid blunders and ignominious defeats. In any given present moment, the greatest coaches live in agonizing ambiguity.

Robert Wuthnow describes the third principle of the Benedictine Rule as "a commitment to live faithfully in unsettled times and to keep one's life sufficiently un-settled to respond to the changing voice of God."[6] This tenet recognizes the essential vulnerability of the human condition to the greater mystery of God's purposes. Great coaches in sports may rely on the statistical research of their staff, the training of the team, and their experience in sports; but when the decisive moment of the game arrives, they are prepared to renounce it all for the sake of an inspired option. The question that haunts them is whether or not the inspiration is divine. They are accountable for that choice.

The more spiritual leaders surrender to biblical visions, the more God requires them to take ownership for their own success or failure. The more passionately the spiritual leaders surrender their will to God, the more urgently God insists they take their will back again. The more rigorously spiritual leaders apply disci-pline to their lives, the more unsettlingly God disrupts their discipline. The awareness of this dilemma, and the willingness to live within its discomfort, is the difference between modern and postmodern leadership.

The shift from *vision* to *action* is a natural step to take. It is done every day in countless small businesses and large corporations, by governments and social services. It is an easy step, an unthinking step, and a *logical* step for modern people to take. The trouble is, it is no longer a modern world. In a postmodern world that simple, unthinking step has become an act of incredibly auda-cious courage.

Notes

1. From "Chester Forgets Himself" in *The Heart of a Goof* by P. G. Wodehouse (New York: Penguin, 1978), p. 78.
2. *The Oxford Dictionary of the Christian Church*, ed. F. L. Cross (New York: Oxford University Press, 1961), p. 152.

3. Robert Wuthnow, *After Heaven: Spirituality in America Since the 1950's* (Ewing: University of California Press, 1998), pp. 5-6.

4. *Christian Spirituality: Origins to the Twelfth Century*, ed. Bernard McGinn, John Meyendorff, Jean Leclercq (New York: Crossroad, 1988), p. 118.

5. Jean Leclercq, *The Love of Learning and the Desire for God* (Bronx: Fordham University Press, 1974), pp. 14-15.

6. Wuthnow, *After Heaven*, p. 6.

Chapter Ten

So Get Out There and Coach!

Coaches are God's metaphor.
They are a metaphor that casts a metaphor about casting metaphors, so others can be captured by a metaphor.

People seeking to leverage change in the church, or seeking to coach the church to change, need to have a keen sense of the ironic. They, simultaneously, take everything and nothing seriously. One moment they aggrandize themselves, and the next moment they dismiss themselves. Just when spiritual leaders seem most confident, they burst into uncontrollable laughter at their inadequacy. They seem to be aware that God must have an extraordinary sense of humor to choose them as spiritual leaders.

The humility of the spiritual leader who coaches change in the postmodern world is akin to the humility of the monastic who brought change to the medieval world. Humility for such people is not a self-deprecating attitude but an ability to change social roles. The monastic was a political statesman, military commander, renaissance educator, church administrator, and pious servant all in the same lifetime. One moment these medieval agents for change would be stirring the crowd with inspiring oratory, and the next they would be enrapt by a vow of silence. Surely they must have sensed the irony. They must occasionally have laughed out loud at God's sense of humor.

Vision Casting

The only equivalent example that I can find in the twenty-first century for the remarkable humility of the medieval monastic is the ordinary fly fisherman, that solitary individual who wanders off into the woods to isolated streams and reappears to mentor irrational apprentices chanting the mantra of lure, rod, and reel. When spiritual leaders speak of casting visions, they do not refer to ceramics. It is not about pouring clay into static molds to cast a perfect, immovable, timeless sculpture. They refer, I think, to fly fishing. It is about casting a line into a distant pool to see who bites.

Earlier I challenged church leaders to make the hard decision for mission rather than maintenance—fully conscious that either way you would lose some people: fish or cut bait. Perhaps by the time you have finished this book, you will have decided that you would rather *fish*. Instead of lamenting with your buddies in the lodge about all the fish that got away, you will leave your buddies behind and go out to be a "fisher of humanity" for Christ. Here is a quick summary of what it will require of you:

1. *It requires imaginative self-discipline.* Fly fishermen imagine the wildest lures, then spend hours squinting into a creative moment to tie the fly. Even so, the spiritual leaders must bring remarkable discipline to their imagination, creating out of culture a hook of singular practicality.

2. *It requires lifestyle commitment.* Fly fishermen shape
    their whole lives around the right afternoon to go
    fishing and, in the meantime, search everywhere for
    the right equipment and blow the budget on the best
    gear. Even so, spiritual leaders shape their lifestyles
    around casting visions. They follow no strategic plan
    but await the right moment and, in the meantime,
    search for the right technologies and resources so
    that when the moment comes they are ready.

3. *It requires intuitive discernment.* When the right after-
    noon comes, fly fishermen go out to the river and
    intuitively discern the right pool in which to cast the
    line. Science will not suffice. The right depth, the
    right color, the right water movement, the right veg-
    etation, the right sunlight or shade—these are all
    variables that can only be discerned by a fly fisher-
    man's art. Even so, when the right moment comes,
    the spiritual leader intuitively discerns the person,
    the neighborhood, and the cultural context toward
    which to cast the vision. Demographic research will
    not suffice. The right context has so many variables
    that discernment can only be an art.

4. *It requires a readiness to risk.* Fly fishermen know that
    they are casting a very sharp hook. If any creature is
    in the way, it may get hurt. If any bush is in the way,
    the line may become tangled, and the act of untan-
    gling it may puncture the fishermen's flesh. Even so,
    spiritual leaders know they are casting a very
    pointed vision. They can hurt people. They can
    become entangled in culture, and the subsequent
    rescue may puncture flesh and make them bleed.

5. *It requires repetitive patience:* Fly fishermen throw the
    line over and over and over and over again. They are

never discouraged. Each time the cast is made with the same fresh energy and hope as the time before. Even so, spiritual leaders cast the vision over and over again, never discouraged when it comes back empty. Each time they are hopeful, confident that if it is God's vision, it will ultimately bear fruit.

6. *It requires intense concentration.* Fly fishermen are indifferent to the mosquitoes and the weather. The beauty of the forest is admired, but it does not hold their gaze. They are constantly correcting mistakes, improving each cast, arcing each line more gracefully, and placing each hook more perfectly. Even so, spiritual leaders must be indifferent to the nuisances and obstacles that regularly block mission. Concentration must not waver. The pleasures of life may be enjoyed, but they must not be allowed to distract.

7. *It requires audacity.* Fly fishermen actually believe they can catch a fish. Endless wading in cold water, uncountable casts into distant pools, nothing diminishes her or his inscrutable optimism. If the time is not right, a better time will come. If the equipment, the cast, or the lures are imperfect, they can be improved. No matter how many times they return empty-handed, after a little more tinkering they will venture forth again. Even so, spiritual leaders are convinced that the vision they cast will eventually capture another human heart.

8. *It requires satisfaction with small victories.* Fly fishermen are not out to catch an ocean of fish, just one trout. It does not have to be a whale, it can be a carp. The number and the size can increase, but fly fishermen catch one fish at a time. Even so, spiritual lead-

ers are not disappointed by small congregations. Big visions grow one step at a time.

9. *It requires irrational joy.* Fly fishermen must be able to experience profound serenity and unbounded excitement standing all alone in the middle of nowhere. Where have they come from? It doesn't matter. Where are they going? They aren't sure. All they know is they stand knee deep in the place where they should be. Even so, spiritual leaders need to find serenity and joy in what seems to be a wasteland or a wilderness. Their tradition or denominational heritage does not matter. Their ultimate career path may be uncertain. All they know is they are at the place and time they are meant to be.

10. *It requires incredible desire.* Fly fishermen know that an inadvertent step will fill their wading boots with water and threaten drowning and that they may cast the line all their lives and never catch a fish. So why do it? Because they *want* to! Even so, spiritual leaders desire to be with God in the cultural wilderness above all else. Their personal fulfillment lies in the experience. Their life expectancy hangs in the balance. In the end, it is not a desire to fish that takes them into the cultural wilderness. It is a desire to be with God.

The true fly fisherman is not particularly worried that his buddies at the lodge will miss or resent him. His worry is that, tucked away in that comfortable lodge, he might have missed God.

In the fullness of God's plan for the postmodern world, the spiritual leaders who cast the visions are themselves God's "bait" to lure new apostles into the mission field. Their imagination, self-discipline, commitment, intuition, readiness to risk, incredible patience, intense concentration, crazy audacity, indifference to size, and irrational joy inspire and coach others about the glories of true Christian discipleship.

And who knows? Maybe their buddies back at the lodge will take the bait, forsake the lodge, pick up their poles, and wade back into the torrent that is God's millennial mission.